To The Reader

This book is presented in its original form and is part of the religious literature and works of Scientology® Founder, L. Ron Hubbard. It is a record of Mr. Hubbard's observations and research into the nature of man and each individual's capabilities as a spiritual being, and is not a statement of claims made by the author, publisher or any Church of Scientology.

Scientology is defined as the study and handling of the spirit in relationship to itself, universes and other life. Thus, the mission of the Church of Scientology is a simple one: to help the individual regain his true nature, as a spiritual being, and thereby attain an awareness of his relationship with his fellow man and the universe. Therein lies the path to personal integrity, trust, enlightenment, and spiritual freedom itself.

Scientology and its forerunner and substudy, Dianetics, as practiced by the Church, address only the "thetan" (spirit), which is senior to the body, and its relationship to and effects on the body. While the Church is free, as all churches are, to engage in spiritual healing, its primary goal is increased spiritual awareness for all. For this reason, neither Scientology nor Dianetics is offered as, nor professes to be physical healing, nor is any claim made to that effect. The Church does not accept individuals who desire treatment of physical or mental illness but, instead, requires a competent medical examination for physical conditions, by qualified specialists, before addressing their spiritual cause.

The Hubbard® Electrometer, or E-Meter, is a religious artifact used in the Church. The E-Meter, by itself, does nothing and is only used by ministers and ministers-in-training, qualified in its use, to help parishioners locate the source of spiritual travail.

The attainment of the benefits and goals of the Scientology religion requires each individual's dedicated participation, as only through one's own efforts can they be achieved.

We hope reading this book is only one step of a personal voyage of discovery into this new and vital world religion.

This Book Belongs To

THE
PROBLEMS
OF WORK
Scientology Applied to the Workaday World

THE
PROBLEMS
OF WORK

Scientology Applied to the Workaday World

L. RON HUBBARD

Bridge
Publications, Inc.

A
HUBBARD®
PUBLICATION

BRIDGE PUBLICATIONS, INC.
4751 Fountain Avenue
Los Angeles, California 90029

ISBN 978-1-4031-4426-3

SCIENTOLOGY: A system of organized axioms resolving problems of the spirit, life and thought, developed through the application of the methodology of the exact sciences to the humanities by L. Ron Hubbard.

The term *Scientology* is taken from the Latin *scio* (knowing, in the fullest meaning of the word) and the Greek word *logos* (study of). Scientology is further defined as the study and handling of the spirit in relationship to itself, universes and other life.

DIANETICS: A forerunner and substudy of Scientology.

Dianetics comes from the Greek words *dia* (through) and *nous* (mind or soul). Dianetics is what the soul is doing to the body.

IMPORTANT NOTE

In reading this book, be very certain you never go past a word you do not fully understand. The only reason a person gives up a study or becomes confused or unable to learn is because he or she has gone past a word that was not understood.

The confusion or inability to grasp or learn comes AFTER a word the person did not have defined and understood. It may not only be the new and unusual words you have to look up. Some commonly used words can often be misdefined and so cause confusion.

This datum about not going past an undefined word is the most important fact in the whole subject of study. Every subject you have taken up and abandoned had its words which you failed to get defined.

Therefore, in studying this book be very, very certain you never go past a word you do not fully understand. If the material becomes confusing or you can't seem to grasp it, there will be a word just earlier that you have not understood. Don't go any further, but go back to BEFORE you got into trouble, find the misunderstood word and get it defined.

GLOSSARY

To aid reader comprehension, L. Ron Hubbard directed the editors to provide a glossary. This is included in the Appendix, *Editor's Glossary of Words, Terms and Phrases*. Words sometimes have several meanings. The *Editor's Glossary* only contains the definitions of words as they are used in this text. Other definitions can be found in standard language or Dianetics and Scientology dictionaries.

If you find any other words you do not know, look them up in a good dictionary.

THE PROBLEMS OF WORK

CONTENTS

INTRODUCTION

Scientology, THE BROAD science of Life, has many applications.

If you knew what life was doing, you would know what many sciences and activities were doing.

Here, we have Scientology assisting the worker and the executive in assisting Man to be more competent and more able, less tired and more secure in the workaday world.

Scientology is already in use in many of the larger businesses of Earth. They have found they could use it.

L. RON HUBBARD

CHAPTER ONE

ON WHAT DOES HOLDING A JOB DEPEND?

ON WHAT DOES HOLDING A JOB DEPEND?

ON WHAT DOES HOLDING A job depend?

Familial connections? Who you know? Personal charm? Luck? Education? Industry? Interest? Intelligence? Personal ability?

To one grown old and even somewhat cynical in the world of work, the first several seem to have dominance. Only the young appear to be left with the illusion or delusion that personal ability, intelligence, interest, education and industry have anything to do with it. And the very, very cynical would have us believe that, indeed, these are only the symptoms of being very young.

We have too often seen the son become the foreman, the new son-in-law, yesterday the shipping clerk, soar to board membership. And we all too often have known that the son and son-in-law not only had no aptitude in the first place but, with no fear of discipline, acted more carelessly of the firm than the worst employee present. Familial connection is something dependent upon the accident of what one is born–an accident rather than, too often happens, a condemnation to involuntary lineage.

But leaving familial connection until some other day, what have we left?

There is who you know. Personal connection plays a dominant part in obtaining, keeping and improving a position. There can be no doubt of this. One has a friend who works for the Jim-Jambo Company, the friend knows of an opening, the friend has other friends and these still other friends—and so into Jim-Jambo Company one can settle down and work with some security and hope of rise.

And then there is the matter of personal charm. How often have we seen the young stenographer who couldn't spell "cat" suddenly soar, with her typing fingers still all thumbs, to the post of executive secretary to the boss wherein, while she can't spell "cat" any better, she can certainly spell "rise" and rise again and perhaps even "supper club" or "diamond necklace." And we have also seen the young man with a good "front" soar above his elders because he could perhaps tell the right joke or play a slightly worse game of golf.

We have seen, too, the factor of education all gone awry in firms and governments where the trained man, at how much cost of eyesight, becomes learned beyond credit—yet passed over for some chap who didn't have a degree to his name beyond a certain degree of push. We have seen the untutored madly ordering the millions and the wise advising a score.

Industry, as well, seems to have scant place to those cynical few of us who have seen it all. The eagerness of the young to slave is all too often braked by the older head who says, "Why get in a sweat about it, young 'un? It'll all come out the same." And perhaps we've stayed after hours and daubed ourselves with ink or lingered at our post beyond all demand of duty, only to watch, in times to come, the lazy one we scorned draw the better pay. And we've said it isn't justice—something less than that.

And interest, too, we've seen come all to naught. When our absorption in the deadly game of "firm or unit with its rivals" made us lay aside neglected our own wife or life, and when we've burned the night and leisure time to work out solutions gauged to save our firm, and have sent them in and have had them come back, neglected, and soon have beheld our fellow worker, whose total interest was a man or "stamps" and not the firm at all, go up to higher posts—we had some cause to be less interested, we thought. And interest in our work became condemned by those around us who, not understanding it, became tired of hearing it in our mouths.

Intelligence, against this hard-beaten parade of broken illusions, would seem to have no bearing whatever upon our fates. When we see the stupid rule the many, when we see the plans and decisions passed that would have been condemned even by the children of the workers, we wonder what intelligence could have to do with it. Better to be dumb, we might come to think, than have our own wits continually outraged by the stupidities which pass for company planning.

Personal ability, against this torrent, this confusing chaos of random causes for promotion and better pay, would seem a wasted item. We have seen our own wasted. We have seen the abilities of others scorned. We have seen the unable rise while the able remained neglected or even unemployed. So personal ability would not seem the factor it might once have been to us, small cogwheels in the clashing gears of business fate. It must, then, certainly be luck and nothing but luck the whole way down.

And so it seems to appear, even to an "experienced" eye, that the obtaining, the holding and the improving of a job are all dependent upon a chaos of causes, all of them out of our control. We accept, instead of orderly expectancy, a tumbling mass of "accidentals" as our fate.

We try a little. We dress well and cleanly in order to apply for a position, we take ourselves to the place of work daily, we shuffle the papers or the boxes or the machinery parts in a fashion we hope will pass, we leave by crowded transport to our homes and expect another day's dull toil.

Occasionally we start up a correspondence course to give us a small edge on our fellows—and often drop it before it is done. It seems that we cannot even do this little to help us on our way against this flood of accidentals.

We become ill. We run out of sick leave. Still but hardly recovered, we now have no job. We become the victims of an accidental cabal or slander and we have no job. We are thrust up against jobs we cannot do and then again we have no job. We grow too old, our time is spent in remembering how fast we once were, and one day we have no job.

The lot of the man in the workaday world is *uncertainty*. His goal is *security*. But only few attain that goal. The rest of us worry from day to day, from year to year, about our ability to get work, hold work, improve our lots. And all too often our worst fears take place.

Once we had the rich to look toward and envy. But now the taxes which we bear have reduced, despite their clever accountants, even their number. States and governments rise and promise us all security and then give us restrictions which make that seem shaky too.

From day to day new threats impose themselves on our consciousness. A world where the machine is king makes Man a cog. And we are told of new developments which do the work of thousands of us and so we starve.

The advertisements thrust at us—in our transports, newspapers, streets, radios and TV—all manner of things to own.

"A world where the machine is king makes
Man a cog. And we are told of new developments
which do the work of thousands of us and so we starve."

And no matter how delightful they are to own *we,* the men who make them, can't own them—not on our pay. And Christmases leave us a little ashamed at how little we can buy and we make the coat do just another year. And the years advance and we grow no younger. And each hour confronts us with the accidents which might make or break our futures. No wonder we believe in *luck* alone.

Well, there is the problem.

To eat we must have a job. To live we must continue to be acceptable on our jobs. To better ourselves we must hope for the breaks. And it all appears a huge, disheartening confusion composed of accidents, good luck and bad luck, or drudgery with nothing to win at the end of it.

What would you give for something to lift you out of such ruts? Perhaps you are not in them. But if not, you're one of the lucky ones. Men, to escape these ruts, have perpetrated the bloodiest wars and revolutions of history. Whole dynasties have been cut to dust in an overpowering convulsion born from despair. Jobs get few. Holding them becomes more and more accidental. At last none can longer stand the strain of insecurity and the answer is raw, red revolution. And does this come to anything? No. Revolution is that act of displacing a tyranny with a tyranny ten times more despotic than the old. Changing governments, not even changing firms, can change basic security.

The quest for security is a quest for constancy and peace. A worker deserves these things. He creates the goods. He should have the wherewithal to live. Instead, he has a chaos.

But where is this chaos? Is it in the worker's family? Some say so. Is it in the character of capital? Some say so. Is this chaos born of bad government? Many have said so. Is it in the worker himself? Some would like him to think that.

No, it is not in any of these things. The chaos of insecurity exists in the chaos of data about work and about people. If you have no compasses by which to steer through life, you get lost. So many recent elements—of the Industrial Age—have entered into life that life itself needs to be better understood.

Work and security are parts of life. If life is not understood, then neither will these parts of life be understood. If all life seems chaotic, a matter of guess and chance, then certainly work will seem chaotic.

But the role of work in existence is the greater role than any other. Some say we spend a third of our lives in bed and therefore beds are important. But we spend more than a third of our lives at work. And if we don't work, we don't have a bed. So it seems that work is more important by far. If you add up the various parts of life, love or sports or entertainment, you will find that the majority of concentration is not on any of these but upon *work*. Work is the major role of our existences whether we like it or not. If we don't like it, we don't like life.

If we find a man a bit insane, old time -ologies would have had us look up his love life or his childhood. A newer idea and a better one is to look up his security and conditions of work. As security goes bad in a nation, insanity rises. If we were to attack national insanity problems and conquer them, we wouldn't build better insane asylums—we would better the condition of work.

Life is seven-tenths work, one-tenth familial, one-tenth political and one-tenth relaxation. Economics—the paycheck, struggle for—is seven-tenths of existence. Lose a man his income or his job and you find him in bad mental condition, usually. If we're going to find proofs of this anywhere, we'll find them everywhere.

Worry over security, worry over worth, worries about being able to do things in life for others are the principal worries of existence.

Let's be very simple. People with nothing to do, people without purpose, most easily become neurotic or mad. Work, basically, is not a drudgery. It is something to do. The paycheck tells us we are worth something. And, of course, it buys us what we have to have to live. Or almost does.

All right. Work security, then, is important. But security itself is an understanding. Insecurity is *unknownness*. When one is insecure, he simply doesn't know. He is not sure. Men who *know* are secure. Men who don't know believe in luck. One is made insecure by not knowing whether or not he is going to be sacked. Thus he worries. And so it is with all insecurity.

INSECURITY EXISTS IN THE ABSENCE OF KNOWLEDGE.

All security derives from knowledge. One *knows* he will be cared for no matter what happens. That is a security. In the absence of certain knowledge it could also be a fallacy.

Luck is chance. To depend upon luck is to depend upon not-knowingness.

But, in truth, how could one have knowledge about life when life itself had not been brought, as knowledge, into order? When the subject of life itself was a chaos, how could work, as a part of life, be anything but a chaos?

If *livingness* is an unknown subject, then *workingness* and all pertaining to work must be an unknown subject, exposed to cynicism, hopelessness and guesses.

To obtain, hold and improve a job, one would have to know the exact, precision rules of life if one were to have a complete security. It would not be enough to know fairly well one's job.

*"Insecurity exists in the
absence of knowledge."*

That would not be a security, for as time went on we would see—as we have listed—too many chances entering into it.

Knowledge of the general underlying rules of life would bring about a security of life. Knowledge of the underlying rules of life would also bring about a security in a job.

Scientology is a science of life. It is the first entirely Western effort to understand life. All earlier efforts came from Asia or Eastern Europe. And they failed. None of them gave greater security. None of them could change human behavior for the better. None of them—and they bragged about it—could change human intelligence. Scientology is something new under the sun. But, young as it is, it is still the only completely and thoroughly tested and validated science of existence. It doesn't demand twenty years of sitting on spikes to find out one is mortal. It doesn't demand a vast study of rats to know that Man is confused.

Scientology can, and does, change human behavior for the better. It puts the individual under the control of himself—where he belongs. Scientology can, and does, increase human intelligence. By the most exact tests known, it has been proven that Scientology can greatly increase intelligence in an individual. And Scientology can do other things. It can reduce reaction time and it can pull the years off one's appearance. But there is no intention here to give a list of all it can do. It is a science of life and it works. It adequately handles the basic rules of life and it brings order into chaos.

A science of life would be, actually, a science of good order. Such things as accidents and luck would, if you could but understand their underlying principles, be under your control.

As we have seen here, even those who aren't cynical can see that many chances enter into obtaining, holding and improving one's job. Some of those chances seem so wide and out of control that nothing at all could be done about them.

But if we could but reduce the chanciness of a job, if we could make the right friends and be sure that our education would count and have some slight security that our interest and intelligence and native ability would not go all to waste—why, then, things would be better, wouldn't they?

Well, we'll see what Scientology can do to reduce the chanciness of the workaday world—for you and for those you know.

What's life all about anyway?

CHAPTER TWO

HANDLING THE
CONFUSIONS OF THE
WORKADAY WORLD

HANDLING THE CONFUSIONS OF THE WORKADAY WORLD

WE HAVE SEEN HOW ONE might be led to believe there was something confusing about navigating one's career in the world of work. And confusion there is to one who is not equipped with guides and maps.

Basically, it all seemed very simple, this thing called work, getting a job. One was educated into some skill and one read an ad or was sent by a friend and was interviewed for a job. And one got it and then reported every day and did the things assigned and, as time went on, hoped for a raise in pay. And time going even further on brought one to hope for a pension or a governmental regime that would pay old-age benefits. And that was the simple pattern of it.

But times change and simple patterns have a habit of being deranged. The various incidents and accidents of fate entered into the picture. Completely aside from personal factors, larger views alter things. The government in sweeping economy fails to grant adequate pension. The business for which one works is shattered by a time of depression. Or one's health fails inexplicably and one is left on charity.

The worker in his workaday world is no towering giant amongst his many foes. The "tinsel path" sketched so happily by "rabble-rousers," the great affection held for the worker by this or that ideology or political figure, do not reflect fact. A man working at a job is faced by difficulties large enough to him, no matter how small they might seem to a successful industrialist. A few percent rise in taxes may mean that he thereafter goes without simple pleasures. An entrance upon bad times for the business may result in lessened pay, and there may go any and all luxuries and even some necessities—or the job.

The effect of international currents, governments, business trends and markets all usually beyond his concern, the worker is perfectly entitled to believe that his fate is not quite entirely predictable. Indeed, he might even be entitled to be confused.

A man can starve to death in a few days. Few workers have many days of margin in their pockets if the currents change. Thus many things, which would be no vast problem to the very secure, are watched as menaces by the worker. And these things can become so many that all life seems too confused to be borne and one sinks into an apathy of day-to-day grind, without much hope, trusting that the next storm, by luck, will pass over him.

As one looks at the many factors which might derange his life and undermine his security, the impression of "confusion" seems well founded. And it can be said, with truth, that all difficulties are fundamentally confusions. Given enough menace, enough unknown, a man ducks his head and tries to swing through it blindly. He has been overcome by confusions.

Enough unsolved problems add up to a huge confusion. Every now and then, on his job, enough conflicting orders bring the worker into a state of confusion. A modern plant can be so poorly managed that the entire thing appears to be a vast confusion to which no answer is possible.

Luck is the usual answer one resorts to in a confusion. If the forces about one seem too great, one can always "rely on his luck." By luck we mean "destiny not personally guided." When one turns loose an automobile wheel and hopes the car will stay on the road, by luck, he is often disappointed. And so it is in life. Those things left to chance become less likely to work themselves out.

One has seen a friend shutting his eyes to the bill collectors and gritting his teeth while he hopes that he will win at the races and solve all his problems. One has known people who handled their lives this way for years. Indeed, one of Dickens' great characters had the entire philosophy of "waiting for something to turn up." But luck, while we grant that it *is* a potent element, is only necessary amid a strong current of confusing factors. If one has to have *luck* to see him through, then it follows that one isn't any longer at his own automobile wheel. And it follows, too, that one is dealing with a confusion.

A confusion can be defined as "any set of factors or circumstances which do not seem to have any immediate solution."

More broadly:

A CONFUSION IN THIS UNIVERSE IS RANDOM MOTION.

If you were to stand in heavy traffic, you would be likely to feel confused by all the motion whizzing around you. If you were to stand in a heavy storm with leaves and papers flying by, you would be likely to feel confused.

Is it possible to actually understand a confusion? Is there any such thing as an "anatomy of confusion"? Yes, there is.

If, as a switchboard operator, you had ten calls hitting your board at once, you might feel confused. But is there any answer to the situation?

If, as a shop foreman, you have three emergencies and an accident all at the same time, you might feel confused. But is there any answer to that?

A confusion is only a confusion so long as *all* particles are in motion. A confusion is only a confusion so long as *no* factor is clearly defined or understood.

Confusion is the basic cause of stupidity. To the stupid, all things except the very simple ones are confused. Thus, if one knew the anatomy of confusion, no matter how bright one might be, he would be brighter.

If you have ever had to teach some young aspirant who was not too bright, you will understand this well. You attempt to explain how such-and-so works. You go over it and over it and over it. And then you turn him loose and he promptly makes a complete botch of it. He "didn't understand," he "didn't grasp it." You can simplify your understanding of his misunderstanding by saying, very rightly, "He was confused."

Ninety-nine percent of all education fails, when it fails, on the grounds that the student was confused. And not only in the realm of the job, but in life itself. When failure approaches, it is born, one way or another, from confusion. To learn of machinery or to live life, one has to be able either to stand up to confusion or to take it apart.

We have, in Scientology, a certain doctrine about confusion. It is called:

THE DOCTRINE OF THE STABLE DATUM.

If you saw a great many pieces of paper whirling about a room, they would look confused until you picked out *one* piece of paper to be *the* piece of paper by which everything else was in motion. In other words, a confusing motion can be understood by conceiving one thing to be motionless.

*"A confusion is only a confusion so long
as all particles are in motion."*

In a stream of traffic, all would be confusion unless you were to conceive *one* car to be motionless in relation to the other cars and so to see others in relation to the one.

The switchboard operator, receiving ten calls at once, solves the confusion by labeling—correctly or incorrectly—*one* call as the first call to receive her attention. The confusion of "ten calls all at once" becomes less confusing the moment she singles out one call to be answered.

The shop foreman, confronted by three emergencies and an accident, needs only to elect his *first* target of attention to start the cycle of bringing about order again.

Until one selects *one* datum, *one* factor, *one* particular in a confusion of particles, the confusion continues. The *one* thing selected and used becomes the *stable datum* for the remainder.

Any body of knowledge, more particularly and exactly, is built from *one datum*. That is its *stable datum*. Invalidate it and the entire body of knowledge falls apart. A stable datum does not have to be the correct one. It is simply the one that keeps things from being in a confusion and on which others are aligned.

Now, in teaching a young aspirant to use a machine, he failed to grasp your directions, if he did, because he lacked a stable datum. *One fact* had to be brought home to him first. Grasping that, he could grasp others. One is stupid, then, or confused in any confusing situation until he has fully grasped *one fact* or *one item.*

Confusions, no matter how big and formidable they may seem, are composed of data or factors or particles. They have pieces. Grasp *one* piece or locate it thoroughly. Then see how the others function in relation to it and you have steadied the confusion. And relating *other* things to what you have grasped, you will soon have mastered the confusion in its entirety.

In teaching a boy to run a machine, don't throw a torrent of data at him and then point out his errors—that's confusion to him, that makes him respond stupidly. Find some entrance point to his confusion, *one datum*. Tell him, "This is a machine." It may be that all the directions were flung at someone who had no real certainty, no real order in existence. "This is a machine," you say. Then make him sure of it. Make him feel it, fiddle with it, push at it. "This is a machine," tell him. And you'd be surprised how long it may take, but you'd be surprised as well how his certainty increases. Out of all the complexities he must learn to operate it, he must know *one datum* first. It is not even important *which* datum he first learns well, beyond that it is better to teach him a *simple basic datum.* You can show him what it does, you can explain to him the final product, you can tell him why *he* has been selected to run this machine. *But* you *must* make one basic datum clear to him or else he will be lost in confusion.

Confusion is *uncertainty*. Confusion is *stupidity*. Confusion is *insecurity*. When you think of uncertainty, stupidity and insecurity, think of confusion and you'll have it down pat.

What, then, is *certainty?* Lack of confusion. What, then, is *intelligence?* Ability to handle confusion. What, then, is *security?* The ability to go through or around or to bring order to confusion. Certainty, intelligence and security are *lack of* or *ability to handle* confusion.

How does luck fit into confusion? Luck is the hope that some uncontrolled chance will get one through. Counting on luck is an abandonment of control. That's apathy.

There is "good control" and "bad control." The difference between them is *certainty* and *uncertainty*. Good control is certain, positive, predictable. Bad control is uncertain, variable and unpredictable. With good control, one can be certain. With bad control, one is never certain.

A foreman who makes a rule effective today but not tomorrow, who makes George obey but not James, is exercising bad control. In that foreman's wake will come uncertainty and insecurity, no matter what his personal attributes may be.

Because there can be so much uncertain, stupid control, some of us begin to believe that all control is bad. But this is very far from true. Control is necessary if one would bring any order into confusions. One must be able to control things, his body, his thoughts, at least to some degree, to do anything whatever.

A confusion could be called an "uncontrolled randomness." Only those who can exert some control over that randomness can handle confusions. Those who cannot exert control actually breed confusions.

The difference between good and bad control then becomes more obvious. The difference between good and bad, here, is *degree.* A thorough, positive control can be predicted by others. Therefore it is good control. A non-positive, sloppy control cannot be predicted. Therefore it is a bad control. Intention also has something to do with control. Control can be used for constructive purposes or destructive purposes. But you will discover that when destructive purposes are *intended,* bad control is used.

Thus there is a great deal to this entire subject of *confusion.* You may find it rather odd for confusion itself to be used here as a target. But you will find that it is an excellent common denominator to all that we consider evil in life. And if one can become master of confusions, his attention is freed for *constructive* activity. So long as one is being confused by confusions, all he can think about are *destructive* things—what he wants to do *most* is to destroy the confusion.

So let us then learn first how to destroy confusions. And this we find is a rather simple thing.

When *all* particles seem to be in motion, halt one and see how the others move according to *it* and then you will find less confusion present. With *one* adopted as a *stable datum,* others can be made to fall in line. Thus an emergency, a machine, a job or life itself can be viewed and understood and one can be free.

Let us take a glance at how this works. In the first chapter we listed a number of things which might influence obtaining, holding and improving a job. One can handle this entire problem, as people most often do, by entering into the problem the single datum, "I can get and hold a job." By clutching to this as a single belief, the confusions and insecurities of life become less effective, less confusing.

But suppose one has done this: Without further investigating the problem, one, when young, gritted his teeth and shut his eyes and said, "I can get and hold a job, come what may. Therefore I am not going to worry about the economics of existence anymore." Well, that was fine.

Later on, without warning, one got fired. One was out of work for ten weeks. He felt then, even when he did get a new job, less secure, less confident. And let us say that some accident occurred and one was out of a job again. When once more unemployed, he was once more even less confident, less secure. Why?

Let us take a look at the opposite side of this Doctrine of the Stable Datum. If we do, we learn that confusions are held ineffective by stable data and that when the stable datum is shaken, the confusion comes into being again.

Let us envision a confusion as stopped. It is still scattered, but it is stopped. What stopped it? The adoption of a stable datum. Let us say that one was bothered badly in the home by a mother-in-law. One day, after a quarrel, one stalked out and by inspiration said to himself, "All mothers-in-law are evil."

That was a decision. That, rightly or wrongly, was a stable datum adopted in a confusion. At once one felt better. He could deal with or live with the problem now. He knew that "All mothers-in-law were evil." It wasn't true, but it was a stable datum.

Then one day, when he was in trouble, his mother-in-law stepped forward, true-blue, and paid not only the rent but the other debt too. At once he felt very confused. This act of kindness should not have been a thing to bring in confusion. After all, hadn't she solved the problem? Then why does one feel upset about it? *Because the stable datum has been shaken.* The entire confusion of the past problem came into action again by reason of the demonstrated falsity of the stable datum.

To make anyone confused, all you have to do is locate their stable data and invalidate them. By criticism or proof, it is only necessary to shake these few stable data to get all a person's confusions back into action.

You see, stable data do not have to be *true*. They are simply *adopted*. When adopted, then one looks at other data in relation to them. Thus the adoption of *any* stable datum will tend to nullify the confusion addressed. *But* if that stable datum is shaken, invalidated, disproven, then one is left again with the confusion. Of course, all one has to do is adopt a new stable datum or put the old stable datum back in place. But he'd have to know Scientology in order to accomplish this smoothly.

Let us say one has no fears of national economy because of a heroic political figure who is trying his best. That man is the stable datum to all one's confusions about national economy. Thus one "isn't worried." But one day, circumstances or his political enemies shake him as a datum. They "prove" he was really dishonest. One then becomes worried all over again about national economy.

Maybe you adopted some philosophy because the speaker seemed such a pleasant chap. Then some person carefully proves to you that the speaker was actually a thief or worse. One adopted the philosophy because one needed some peace from his thoughts. Invalidating the speaker would then at once bring back the confusion one faced originally.

All right. We looked at the confusion of the workaday world when we were young, and we held it all back by stating grimly, "I can get and keep a job." That was the stable datum. We did get a job. But we got fired. The confusion of the workaday world then became very confusing. If we have only the one stable datum, "I can get and keep a job," as our total answer to all the various problems listed in the first chapter, then assuredly one is going to spend some confusing periods in his working life. A far, far better stable datum would be, "I understand about life and jobs. Therefore I can get, hold and improve them."

And that's where we are going in this book.

CHAPTER THREE

IS WORK
NECESSARY?

CHAPTER THREE

IS WORK NECESSARY?

AN UNDERSTANDING OF LIFE is necessary to the living of it. Otherwise life becomes a trap. To so many of us in the workaday world, this trap takes the form of WORK.

If only we didn't have to work, how many delightful things could we do! If only we had some other way of getting money... travel, vacations, new clothes...what a host of things would be ours if only we didn't have to work!

It is almost an educational factor of our society that work, duress of, is the root of our unhappiness. We hear unions and welfare states, as well as individuals, basing all their plea upon a reduction of work. Getting rid of work, by virtue of reduced hours and the introduction of automatic machinery, has become the byword of the mid-twentieth century.

Yet the most disheartening thing which could happen to most of us would be the loss of all future jobs. To be denied the right to work is to be denied any part of the society in which we live.

The rich man's son, the moneyed dowager, neither of them works, neither is sane. When we look for neurosis and folly in our society, we look toward those who do not or cannot work.

When we look over the background of a criminal, we look at "inability to work." Somehow, the right to work seems to be bound up in happiness and the zest of living. And demonstrably, the denial of work is bound up with madness and insanity.

As the amount of automatic machinery increases in our society, so increases the percentile of our people who are insane. Child labor laws, injunctions against overtime, demands for many papers and skills and conditions of being, alike, combine to reduce the amount of work that can be done by an individual.

Have you ever seen a retired man who pined for his desk? Today "the doctrine of limited work" educates us to believe that at such-and-such an age we must stop work. Why is this so popular when we can see for ourselves that the end of work is the end of life in most cases?

Speaking politically for a moment, from the standpoint of sanity, Man more dearly needs the *right to work* than he does an endless number of pretended freedoms. Yet we carefully discourage, in our children and in our society, those people who *make* work. Unless work is made, there will be no work to do. Work is not something that springs ready-made into our sight. Work is something that is created. New inventions, new markets, new systems of distribution must be created and brought into existence as times change and old methods, old markets, old systems become inadequate and wear out. Somebody created the jobs we do. When we work, we either do a job created by ourselves or by another.

It is not enough to coast along in a job. The job, day by day, has to be made by *us,* no matter who created it in the first place.

To work is to participate in the activities of our society. To be refused a part in the activities of our society is to be cast out by it.

Somebody invented the difference between "work" and "play." Play was seen to be something that was interesting. And work was seen to be something that was arduous and necessary and therefore not interesting. But when we have our vacations and go and "play," we are usually very glad to get back to the "daily grind." Play is almost purposeless. Work has a purpose.

In truth, only the constant refusal on the part of the society to give us work results in our distaste of work when it exists. The man who cannot work was forbidden the right to work. When we go back in the history of the notoriously unable-to-work criminal, we find that he was first and foremost convinced that he must not work—he was forbidden to work, whether by his father or mother or school or early life. Part of his education was that he must not work. What was left? Revenge upon the society which refused to let him take part in its activities.

Let us redefine work and play. Play should be called "work without a purpose." It could also be called "activity without purpose." That would make work be defined as "activity with purpose."

Where we have fault to find with working, it grows out of our own fear that we will not be permitted to continue work.

There is nothing wrong with automation, with all this installation of machines to do our work, so long as the powers that be remember to create *additional work* for us. Automation could be a blessing to the whole world, *providing* as many new jobs are invented as were disposed of by machinery. *Then* we'd have production! And if the powers that be didn't fumble their basic economics and created enough money for us to buy all the new products, *there* would be prosperity indeed. So it isn't automation that is at fault. If automation leaves people unemployed, *somebody* wasn't permitted to invent new jobs for us.

Of course, if every new business is flattened by restriction and if every man who would invent work was prohibited from doing so, then and *only* then would automatic machinery bring about our downfall.

Despite the much advertised joys of vacations and endless play, such things have never been other than a curse for Man. The earliest mention of it was by Homer in the Lotus Isles. And didn't that crew go to pieces!

No, definitely there is more to work and working than having to have a paycheck. Of course, there are jobs more interesting than other jobs. Of course, there are positions which are more remunerative than other positions. But when one contrasts the right to have a position with *no* right to have one, then one will choose even the less interesting and poorer-paid tasks.

Did you know that a mad person could be made well simply by getting him convinced that he has some purpose in life? Well, that can happen. It doesn't matter how thin or artificial that purpose may be, mad people can be made sane with it. One instance comes to mind of a crazy girl for whom nothing could be done. That was the point in her case—nothing could be done *for her*. But one night near the asylum an auto accident occurred and an overworked doctor, seeing her near, ordered her to do some things for the victims. She became well. She became a staff nurse. She was never insane thereafter.

Now, no one pretends that we are all mad if we don't work. But it is an astonishing thing that we drift in that direction when we are *forbidden* to labor.

Great revolutions occur out of a mass inability to work. The crowds rebel not because they are angry over "privileges," which they always say, but because they have gone mad having no work. It is truth that revolutions cannot occur when people are all employed.

And it doesn't even matter how arduously they are employed, either. Revolutions occur when people have been too often forbidden to work. They go up in madness and the state often comes down in ruins. *No* revolution ever won anything. Life evolves into a better condition by means of hard work, not by threats.

If automatic machinery threw enough people out of work, even though the machines were producing aplenty, there would be a revolution. Why? Because by robbing them of work, people have been robbed of a purpose in life. When that goes, all goes.

A good purpose, a bad purpose, it does not matter so long as a purpose exists. *Why?*

Now do not think we have strayed very far from the last chapter. We haven't. Here is an understanding of life. Life has certain stable data that *are* the stable data of livingness. Once grasped, then life—and that part of it called work—can be understood.

Life is basically a *created* thing. But it has many elements in it creating against many other elements in it. A confusion occurs whenever two or more things start creating against each other. Thus life, viewed impartially, can seem to be a confusion.

If one were to sit amongst all this livingness, all this creatingness, all this warfare, without any purpose, his existence in its entirety would be fatal. To be part of a universe, a civilization, and yet to have no purpose is the route to madness.

The exertion of energy, the exercise, the time spent, the things done are all of a lower order of importance. Just to have *something to do* and a *reason to do it* exerts a control over life itself. If you have no purpose, you have no purchase on that small first particle necessary to make the whole understandable. Thus life can become a terrible burden.

"If one were to sit amongst all this livingness,
all this creatingness, all this warfare, without any
purpose, his existence in its entirety would be fatal.
To be part of a universe, a civilization, and yet
to have no purpose is the route to madness."

In the United States in the 1930s—and in other lands as well—there was something called a Depression. It came out of a lack of understanding of economics during a period of transition into a machine age. During it a great president saw that work had been denied to his people. He created work. He thought he did it to get money into circulation to buy all the things the country could now make. Therefore, he did not really rescue the bulk of his people from despair. For the work he gave them was to be carelessly done, poorly done. All that was being demanded was time spent on the job. He had a wonderful opportunity to turn a country into a beautiful thing. But the work given had no purpose.

Men who detest one job or another detest it because they can't see where it is going or can't believe they are doing any important thing. They are "working." That is to say, they report and go through motions and draw a paycheck. But they aren't truly a part of the scheme of things. They don't feel they have anything to win.

In our civilization, the *stable datum* to the confusion of existence is *work*. And the *stable datum* of work is *purpose*. Even if the purpose is just "getting a paycheck," it is still purpose.

Any of us probably could do more important things than we are doing. Any of us could use some changes in our tasks. But none of us—and still stay alive and sane—could do without something to do.

When we grow timid in the face of circumstance, it is because our *purposes*, our *stable data*, have been invalidated.

It is, as we have shown, rather easy to knock a person into a state of confusion. All you have to do is locate his stable datum on any subject and shake it. This is a trick we all use.

For instance, we are arguing about economics with a friend. We don't agree with him. We ask him where he got such an idea. He says somebody wrote it in such-and-so. We attack the writer or the paper and discredit it. In other words, we win our argument by shaking his stable datum as nearly as we can find it.

Life is competitive. Many of us forget we are part of a team called Man, in contest with who knows what else to *survive*. We attack Man and attack our friends. In the course of holding a job, it seems only natural that here and there in the organization would be people who were so insecure in their own tasks that they seek to spread insecurity around them.

Having drunk of confusion too deeply, having too few stable data, a person can begin to "dramatize" confusion, to spread it, to consciously try to make everything and everybody confused. One of the favorite targets of such people is the stable datum of work. Although usually such people cannot even do their *own* jobs, they are very anxious to make others tired of *theirs*. They "cut down the competition" by carving up the stable data of others.

Beware these people who come around and inquire "sympathetically" about your health because you look "overworked." It is almost easier to get "overloafed" than overworked. Beware these people who want you to sign a petition to shorten the hours to be spent on the job. The end product of that is no job. And beware, too, the fellow who is always "taking it out of the firm" because the firm "can afford it." Remember, that firm is part yours, no matter if they fire you tomorrow. Such people are trying to pull out from under you the stable datum of work.

If you are afraid of losing your job, it is because you suffer already from too many forbiddings to work. The only way to hold a job is to make it every day, to create it and keep it created.

If you have no wish to create and continue that job, then there must be something at *cross-purposes* with *purpose*. There is something wrong between what you think would be a good purpose and what purpose your job has.

Government jobs are interesting because, so often, nobody seems to care, really, whether the job has purpose or not. Too often the purpose of having a government job is just "to have a government job." Here, in particular, one has to understand about life and work itself. For a government job has to be created *continually* to continue. And if it seems to have no purpose, then one should look over government itself and get at *its* purpose. For the purpose of the government as a whole, in some part, would be the purpose of the job held, no matter how small.

Anyone suffering from a distaste for work must basically have a feeling that he isn't really allowed to work. Thus work is not a stable datum in life. And he must have, as well, some cross-purpose about the purposes of his job. And, too, he usually is associated with people in his job who are trying to make work into something less than tasteful. But he is to be pitied because he is unhappy. He is unhappy because he is confused. Why is he confused? Because he has no stable datum for his *life*.

And a stable datum for life, itself, is the basis of good living as well as good job orientation.

CHAPTER FOUR

THE
SECRET OF
EFFICIENCY

The Secret of Efficiency

What is Control?

Whether one handles a machine the size of a car or as small as a typewriter or even an accounting pen, one is faced with the problems of control. An object is of no use to anyone if it cannot be controlled. Just as a dancer must be able to control his body, so must a worker in an office or a factory be able to control his body, the machines of his work and to some degree the environment around him.

The primary difference between the "worker" in an office or a factory and an "executive" is that the executive controls minds, bodies and the placement of communications, raw materials and products, and the worker controls, in the main, his immediate tools. However, it is far too easy, for those anxious to agitate labor into measures not necessarily good for it and for executives who themselves are anxious for control and anxious about it, to forget that the worker who does not control his materials of work–and who is himself a "controlled factor" only–is practically useless to the plant itself. Both management and labor must be able to control their immediate environment.

The most apparent difference between an executive and a worker is that the executive controls more environment than the worker. To that degree, then, the executive must be more capable than the worker—or the plant or business is doomed to difficulty, if not failure.

What is a good workman? He is one who can positively control his equipment or tools of trade or who can control the communication lines with which he is intimately connected.

What is a bad worker? A bad worker is one who is unable to control the equipment he is supposed to control or the communication lines he is supposed to handle.

People who wish to control others, but who do not wish others to control anything, bring us into a difficulty by establishing a fallacy. That fallacy is that there is such a thing as "bad control." Control is either well done or not done. If a person is controlling something, he is controlling it. If he is controlling it poorly, he is not controlling it. A machine which is being run well is controlled. A machine which is not being run well is not being controlled.

Therefore, we see that bad control is actually a "not-control."

People who tell you that control is bad are trying to tell you that automobile accidents and industrial accidents are good.

Attempted control for bad or covert purposes is harmful. But it carries with it the ingredient of unknowingness. The person who is *attempting* control is actually not controlling. He is simply seeking to control and his efforts are, in the main, indefinite and unpositive—which, of course, are characteristics which control itself does not countenance. When unknowingness is entered into control, control can become antipathetic. But it does not become a fact.

If you have ever covertly controlled your car, you will understand what is meant. If you handled your steering wheel in such a way that the car would not "know" which way it was then supposed to go, you would soon be involved in difficulties. You must handle the steering wheel of a car in such a way that the car then turns the proper turns and remains on a straight course on a straight road. There is nothing hidden about your intention of controlling the car and there is nothing unknown about the response of the car. When a car fails to respond to your handling of the steering wheel, control has ceased to exist.

In other words, one either controls something or he does not. If he does not, we have developed a misnomer. We have developed the idea that there is such a thing as "bad control."

People who have been "badly controlled" (which is to say, who have been merely shaken up and have not been controlled at all) begin to believe there is something bad about control. But they would really not know what control is since they have not been controlled in actuality.

To understand this further, one would have to know one of the very basic principles of Scientology, which is:

THE ANATOMY OF CONTROL.

In part, this principle consists as follows. Control may be subdivided into three separate parts. These parts are:

START-CHANGE-and-STOP.

Start-change-and-stop also comprise a:

CYCLE-OF-ACTION.

The cycle-of-action is seen in the turning of a simple wheel. The wheel starts and then any given spot on it changes position and the wheel is stopped. It does not matter how long the wheel is in motion, it still follows this cycle-of-action.

A man walking a short distance starts, changes the position of his body and stops his body. He has, if he does this, completed a cycle-of-action.

On a longer span, a company starts, continues and at some date, early or late, ceases to exist.

In change we get "change of position in space or change of existence in time." In start we have simply "start." And in stop we have simply "stop." Things may start slowly or rapidly. Things may stop slowly or rapidly. Things may change very rapidly while they are going. Thus the rate of start, the rate of change and the rate of stop have little to do with the fact that a cycle-of-action does consist of start-change-and-stop.

The Ancients referred to this cycle-of-action in a much more detailed fashion. We find the Vedic Hymns talking about a cycle-of-action in this wise: First there is chaos, then from the chaos something emerges (it can be said to have been born), it grows, it persists, it decays and dies and chaos ensues. Although this, in essence, is an inaccurate statement, it is the earliest example of a cycle-of-action.

A modern Scientology example of a cycle-of-action is much more simply stated and is much more accurate. A cycle-of-action is start-change-and-stop. This parallels another cycle-of-action which is that of life itself. The cycle-of-action of *life* is:

CREATION-SURVIVAL-and-DESTRUCTION.

Survival could be said to be any change, whether in size or in age or in position in space. The essence of survival is change. Creation is, of course, starting. Destruction is, of course, stopping.

Thus we have, in Scientology, two very useful cycles-of-action: The first of them being start-change-and-stop and the more detailed one being create-survive-destroy.

Start

Creation

Change

Survival

Stop

Destruction

*"A cycle-of-action is start-change-and-stop. This
parallels another cycle-of-action which is that
of life itself. The cycle-of-action of life is:
Creation-Survival-and-Destruction."*

Start-change-and-stop imply the condition of a being or an object.

Create-survive-destroy imply the intention of life toward objects.

Control consists entirely of starting, changing and stopping. There are no other factors in positive control.

If one can start something, change its position in space or existence in time and stop it—all at will—he can be said to control it, whatever it may be. If one can barely manage to start something, can only with difficulty continue its change of position or existence in time and can only doubtfully stop something, he cannot be said to control it well and, for our purposes, he would be said to be able to control it poorly or dangerously. If he cannot start something, if he cannot change its position in space, if he cannot stop something, then he is definitely not in control of it. If he is trying to start, change and stop something or somebody without positively doing so, he has entered unknowingness into the activity and the result will be questionable, to say the least.

Thus there is such a thing as "good control." Good control would consist of knowingness and positiveness. A girl who can start a typewriter, continue its motion and then stop it, could be said to be in control of the typewriter. If she had difficulties in starting it, in continuing its action and in stopping it, she would not only be in "bad control" of the typewriter—she would be a bad stenographer.

Where bad control enters in, so enter incompetence, accidents, difficulties, disobedience, inefficiency and, not the least, considerable misery and unhappiness. As we define bad control as "not-control" or as "an unknowing attempt at control without actually effecting control," it can be said that unpositiveness results in a great many difficulties.

To give you some idea of how far this might go in life, you might get the idea of being moved around in a room by somebody. This somebody would tell you to go to the desk, then would tell you to go to a chair, then would tell you to go to the door. Each time he tells you to go somewhere, you of course have to start yourself, change your body's position and stop yourself. Now, oddly enough, you would not mind this if you knew that somebody was telling you to do it and you were capable of performing the action and you were not receiving orders in such a wise as to interrupt your obedience of the command before you completed it.

But let us say, for instance, that somebody told you to go to the desk, but before you arrived at the desk told you to go to a chair, but before you arrived at the chair told you to go to the door and then claimed you were wrong in not having gone to the desk. You would be, at that time, confused. This would be bad control, since it does not permit you to finish any cycle-of-action before another cycle-of-action is demanded of you. Thus your cycles-of-action become involved and a confusion results. But this, in essence, would not be control, since control must involve an understandable or knowing positiveness. Good control would not change the order before you had a chance to arrive at the desk, would let you arrive at the desk before you were asked to start again for the chair and would let you arrive at the chair before you were asked to start again for the door. Now, you would not mind the positive control. But it is certain that you would be quite upset by the broken series of orders which did not permit you to finish any cycle-of-action.

Now, to give you some idea of how this could influence one's life: Which would you rather have give you a series of orders, such as above to move around a room—your father or your mother? It is certain that you had the most trouble with the parent you would *not* have chosen to have given you those orders.

Control is so far from being bad that a person who is sane and in very good condition does not resent good, positive control and is himself able to administer good, positive control to people and objects. A person who is not in very good condition resents even the most casual directions and is actually not capable of controlling people or objects. The latter person is also inefficient and has many difficulties with work and with life.

When a person cannot control things or when he resists things controlling him, he involves himself with difficulties not only with people but with objects. It is also apparent that people with control difficulties more readily become ill and fail in other ways.

When a person is incapable of controlling a piece of machinery, it often occurs that the machinery reverses the matter and begins to control *him*. As an example, a driver who cannot exert positive control on a car is quite likely, eventually, to be controlled by that car. Instead of a driver driving a car down the street, we have a car taking a "driver" down the street. And sooner or later the car, not being very expert at control, winds its driver up in a ditch.

Even mechanical failures are attributable to a lack of control. It will be discovered that an individual who cannot easily control a machine is quite likely to have considerable difficulties with that machine. The machine itself suffers, sometimes in nearly inexplicable ways. Motors run for some men and do not run for others. Some machinery will go on for years in the hands of a mechanic. But when the mechanic leaves it and another takes his place who is not adept, the machine may be found to break down and experience difficulties never before noticed in it. It is stretching things a little bit to infer that a person who cannot control things needs only to look at a piece of machinery to have something go wrong with it. And yet there are cases on record where this has happened.

The factor involved is more easily understood in, for instance, an accounting department. A person who cannot control figures, of course, sooner or later, involves the books he is keeping in complexities and intricacies which not even an expert accountant can straighten.

The cycle-of-action of this universe is start-change-and-stop. And this is also the anatomy of control. Almost the entire subject of control is summed up in the ability to start-change-and-stop one's activities, body and his environment.

A "habit" is simply something one cannot stop. Here we have an example of *no* control whatever. And we have the step, beyond the last extremity, of entirely *lost* control. Control begins to dwindle when one is able to change things and stop things, but is not still capable of *starting* them. Once a thing is started, such a person can change and stop it. A further dwindling of control, if one can now call it such, would be the loss of an ability to *change* something or continue its existence in time. This would leave one simply with the ability to *stop* things. When one finally loses the ability to stop something, that thing has to some degree become his master.

In the *stop* of start-change-and-stop we see, in essence, the entirety of the stable datum. If one can stop just one particle or datum in a confusion of particles or data, one has begun a control of that confusion.

In the matter of a mass of calls coming into a switchboard simultaneously, each call insistently demanding the attention of an operator, control is asserted on the switchboard by the operator's stopping just one demand. It does not particularly matter which demand is stopped. Handling just one call permits one then to handle another call and so forth, until one has changed the condition of the switchboard from a total confusion to a handled situation.

One feels confused when there is nothing in a situation which he can *stop*. When he can at least stop one thing in a situation, he will then find it is possible to stop others and finally will recover the ability to *change* certain factors in the situation. From this he graduates into an ability to change anything in the situation and finally is capable of *starting* some line of action.

Control is then found to be very intimate to confusion.

A worker who is easily confused is a worker who cannot control things. An executive who is frantic in the face of an emergency is an executive who, even in good times, does not feel that he has any ability to actually start-change-and-stop situations in which he is involved as an executive.

Franticness, helplessness, incompetence, inefficiency and other undesirable factors in a job are all traceable to inabilities to start-change-and-stop things.

Let us say that a plant has a good manager. The manager can start-change-and-stop the various activities in which the plant is involved, can start-change-and-stop the various machinery of the plant, can start-change-and-stop the raw materials and the products of the plant and can start-change-and-stop various labor activities or difficulties. But let us say that this plant is unfortunate enough to have only one person in it who can start-change-and-stop things. Now, unless the executive is going to handle all of the incoming raw materials, turn on and off all the machinery, process every piece of material in the place and ship the finished products himself, he will be unable to run the plant.

Similarly, an office manager who himself can start-change-and-stop any of the activities of an office or handle them—if he were the only one in the office who could—would be powerless, actually, to run a very large office.

In a plant or in an office, it is then necessary for an executive, no matter how good he may be, to be supported by subordinates who themselves are not unwilling to be started, changed and stopped by him, but who can themselves start-change-and-stop the activities or personnel in their own immediate environments in the plant.

Now, given a good executive in a plant or office and given good subordinates (defining as "good" their ability to start-change-and-stop things), we would yet have difficulty if we reached lower down on the command chart and discovered that we did not have any working people who themselves were capable of starting, changing and stopping their own particular jobs. We would have a condition, here, where the executive and the foreman would then be forced to do everything that was really being done in the plant. To actually have a good plant, we would have to have an executive, foreman and workers, all of whom in their own environment were capable of starting, changing and stopping things and who were at the same time (including the executive) not unwilling to be started, changed and stopped in their duties—providing positive and understandable orders were used.

As we look this over, we see less and less the picture we have been uniformly presented with in plants and offices of the "management" and "laborers." As soon as we discover one worker in a plant who does not have to start, change or stop himself or anything else, we would then have somebody who would justify this title of "laborer." It is apparent that from the topmost member of the board down to the lowest worker on the payroll, each and every one of them is involved with starting, changing and stopping people, materials, machinery, products and pieces of the environment. In other words, each and every one of them present in a plant or an office is actually managing something.

As soon as an executive realizes this, he is then capable of running a far more efficient business since he is capable, then, of selecting out amongst him people who are best at starting, changing and stopping things. And these, by example, can bring others into a state of mind where they too are willing to positively start-change-and-stop things.

However, in executives, foremen or workers, we have people today who are either stuck on one or another of the factors of control *exclusively* or who are incapable of *any* of the factors of control. Thus we have in any plant, or office or business or activity—even the government—a considerable amount of confusion which would not be present if the people there were capable of controlling what they were supposed to control.

We have people in the workaday world, whether managers or janitors, who are, for instance, fixated (stuck) on *starting*. These people can start all day and all night, but they never get going. Such people talk about big schemes and big deals. Such people talk a lot of enthusiasm about "getting going," but never themselves seem to move.

Others, no matter what their class or classification, get fixated on *change*. These manifest this usually by insisting that everything "keep running." They talk all the time about "keeping things going," but they will not listen to any new ideas or will not receive any new machinery since that would necessitate stopping some old machinery and starting some new machinery. Thus we get antiquated plants and systems continued on forever, long past their usefulness or economic value. A subdivision of this is the person who must *change everything all the time*. This is actually another manifestation of trying to "keep things running." But instead of keeping things running, these people shift everything there is to be shifted all the time. If an order is issued, they change the order. If they receive the word to go, they change it to stay.

But this, it will be seen, is an unbalanced condition—where these people are actually unwilling to keep anything running anywhere and are in reality on an obsessive *stop.*

Plants, businesses, factories, ships and even the government are victimized, particularly, by people who can only *stop* things. No matter how well some unit may be running, some order is issued that stops whatever it is doing. It is enough for such people to discover that something is *going* to do something to cause it to stop. Usually one gets around this by "failing to inform" such people that something is running.

Thus we can see that there are people who abuse the cycle-of-action of start-change-and-stop and who are, themselves, fixated upon *one* or another factor in the cycle-of-action or who are incapable of withstanding *any* factor in it—which means, of course, that they are in a continuous and arduous confusion.

It is noteworthy that those people who can only start things are normally creative. The artist, the writer, the designer is looked upon to start things. He actually might also be capable of continuing them or stopping them, but his purest function is *creation.*

There are, amongst very rational and good men, those whose greatest ability is continuing things. They can also start things and stop things if they can really continue things. It is upon these men that we depend for the *survival* of a business or an operation.

Then there is the class that is used by the society to stop things. Such people have normally a police function. Certain things are declared to be bad and these things so designated are then turned over to people who stop them. Imperfect production is stopped by inspectors. Bribery, corruption or crime is stopped by police. Other national or aggressive persons are stopped by the military. And it should occasion no surprise that these specialists in stop are, of course, specializing in *destroy.*

It should occasion no further surprise that when one looks at the element in a society most likely to decay the society, one looks for those whose job it is to specialize in stops. These people in the main, while serving a very good function for the society at large, if they became fully in charge—as in a police state—would only destroy the state and its people, as has been noted since the days of Napoleon. The most recent nation which turned over the entire function of the state to police was Germany. And Germany was stopped very thoroughly. Germany also effected nothing but destruction.

When we have a society which is very good at starting, we have a creative society. When we have a society which is very good at keeping things running, we have a society which endures. When we have a society which is only capable at stopping things, we have a society which is destructive or which is itself destroyed.

Therefore, we must realize that a balance amongst these three factors of start-change-and-stop is necessary. Not only in an individual, but in a business. And not only in a business, but in a nation. When one can only do one of these, one is considerably limited in his usefulness.

The optimum condition would be for everyone—from manager down to janitor—to be capable of starting, changing and stopping and to be able to endure being started, changed and stopped. Thus we would have a balanced and relatively unconfused business activity. No business can succeed unless it has been properly started, unless it is progressing through time or changing position in space and unless it is capable of stopping harmful practices and even competitors.

As it is with a nation or a business, so it would be with an individual holding down a single job. He should be able to start-change-and-stop anything under his immediate control. If he is running a machine, he should be able to start the machine, to keep it turning (changing) and to stop it. And this should be under his own determinism. His machine should not be started and stopped by some engineer at some period of the day without any attention from himself. Furthermore, if he thought the machine should be shut down and oiled, he should have the authority to do so and should not have to withstand the pummeling of some machine foreman who—without understanding the situation—simply observed that a machine was stopped which, according to his lights, ought to be running.

Even a janitor, to have any efficiency at his job and thus to have a clean set of offices or a plant, would have to be able to start-change-and-stop the various objects having to do with his particular job. He should not have to keep on sweeping after the floor is clean. And he should not have to stop sweeping before he has cleaned the floor. And he should be able to start sweeping the floor when he believes it ought to be swept. Naturally, if he is able to do these things, he is also able to cooperate with his fellow workers and himself be stopped or started or altered in his activity, so as to execute *his* job while making it possible for them to do *their* job.

Here, however, we envision a nation, or a plant or an office or a small section or department, running without any supervision at all. Whereas there would be executives and foremen and workers, it is doubtful if supervision of others would occupy much of anyone's time. As the ability of the worker and foreman and executive to start-change-and-stop those things which they should handle and control declines, it will be discovered that supervision enters in. The less capable people are of starting, changing and stopping the people or objects under their immediate control, the more supervision they require. When supervision gets up to 80 percent of the plant's activities, it is certain that the confusion will be so great that inefficiency will result in such magnitude as to ruin the activity.

Supervision, then, is actually a criticism of the junior. It implies that the junior does not know or is not able in the field of control.

Cooperation and "alignment of activity" is different than supervision. Where one has a chain of command, one does not necessarily have supervision. One does have, however, coordinated planning for an entire operation which is then relayed to others in the operation so that coordination can take place. If everybody is agreed on the worthwhileness of any activity and if everybody in that activity were capable of actually controlling those items or persons which were in his immediate sphere of action, it would be found that planning would not have to engage in much supervision in order to effect the execution of the ideas involved. This is a very high order of dream. Only where Scientology has been thoroughly at work could such a thing occur–that an organization could run in agreement with itself without supervision or punitive action.

One is able to gauge those workers around him by the amount of confusion in which they are involved. That confusion tells one at once the degree of inability to control things. That inability to control things may not be entirely the fault of the worker. There are two things which can be psychotic: One is the surroundings and the other is the person. A sane man has difficulty in insane surroundings. An insane man has difficulty in even the sanest and most orderly surroundings. Thus there are two factors involved in any operation: The person and the surroundings. It could also be said there are two factors involved in any business: The surroundings of the business itself and the business. One sane business trying to operate in a world of madmen would have a very great difficulty getting along. One way or another, the inability of the madmen to start-change-and-stop things would infect the business and deteriorate its efficiency.

Thus it is not enough that an individual himself be capable of controlling his job. He must also be able to tolerate the *confusion* of those around him who cannot control their jobs. Or he must be able to tolerate sane and steady *control* from those around him.

Insanity is contagious. Confusion is contagious. Have you ever talked to a confused man without yourself, at the end of the conversation, feeling a little confused? Thus it is in work. If one is working with a great many men who are incapable, one begins himself to feel incapable. It is not enough to live alone. It is impossible to work alone. Realizing this, one also understands that his ability to control the immediate machinery or work tools with which *he* is involved must also include an ability to assist others in his vicinity to control those things with which *they* are involved.

Many a good worker has been lost to a factory because the good worker could not make his own work good enough to satisfy himself, being faced in his job with so many confused elements and orders that he at last rebelled. Thus good workers can be spoiled. In any department it is possible to spot the people who spoil good workers. They are the people who cannot start-change-and-stop such things as communication or machinery and who are themselves most liable to franticness and confusion. These are the people who would rather have solutions thrown in the wastebasket and problems posted on the bulletin board.

What could one do if he was surrounded by people who were confused and incapable of starting, changing and stopping their various activities?

He could, himself, become sufficiently capable at his own job that he would set a fine example for others and thus, himself, be a stable datum in the confusion of that area.

He could do even more than this. He could understand how to handle men and, so understanding, could bring orderliness into the minds and activities of those men so as to balk their inabilities as they might affect him. But in order to do the latter, he would have to know a great deal about Scientology and its various principles—and that is somewhat beyond the scope of this particular volume.

For the individual worker who wishes to do a good job and to go on having a job and to rise in his position, it is almost enough that he understand his job thoroughly so that no part of it confuses him and so that he can start-change-and-stop anything with which he is connected in that job and that he himself can tolerate being started, changed and stopped by his superiors without himself becoming unsettled. In other words, the greatest asset and greatest job insurance a worker could have would be a *calmness of mind* concerning what he was doing. A calmness of mind is derived from the ability to start-change-and-stop the objects and activities with which he is involved and to be able to be started, changed and stopped by others without himself becoming as confused as they are.

Thus the secret of doing a good job is the secret of control itself. One not only continues to create a job, day by day, week by week, month by month. He also continues the job by permitting it to progress. And he is also capable of stopping or ending any cycle of work and letting it remain finished.

Workers are most often victimized by bosses, juniors or marital partners who are not themselves capable of controlling anything, yet who will not be controlled and who in some peculiar way are obsessed on the idea of control. A worker who is thus intimately connected with something that he himself cannot control, and which is incapable of actually or really controlling him, performs his work in a confused state which can only lead to difficulties and distaste for work itself.

It can be said that the only thing bad about working is that it is so very often associated with inabilities to control. When these are present, then the work itself seems tiresome, arduous and uninteresting and one would rather do anything else than continue that particular work. There are many solutions to this. First amongst them is to regain control of the items or functions which one is most intimately connected with in doing his job.

However, control in itself is not an entire answer to everything. For if it were, one would have to be able to control everything—not only in his own job, but in an office or on Earth—before he could be happy. We discover, in examining control, that the limits of control should be extended only across one's actual sphere of operation. When an individual attempts to extend control far beyond his active interest, in a job or in life, he encounters difficulty. Thus there is a limit to the "area of control" which, if violated, violates many things. It is almost a maxim that if an individual consistently seeks to operate outside his own department, he will not take care of his own department. As a matter of fact, in Scientology organizations it has been discovered that a person who is consistently involving himself with things far *beyond* his actual scope of interest is not covering his *actual* scope of interest.

Thus, there is obviously another factor involved than control. This factor is willingness *not to control* and is fully as important as *control* itself.

CHAPTER FIVE

LIFE
AS A GAME

LIFE
AS A GAME

IT IS QUITE OBVIOUS THAT IF anyone controlled everything, he would have no GAME. There would be no unpredictable factors, no surprises in life. This might be said to be a hell of considerable magnitude.

If one could control everything absolutely, he would of course be able to predict everything absolutely. If he could predict the course and action of every motion in the entirety of existence, he would of course have no real interest in it.

We have already looked at the necessity of controlling the immediate objects of work. But, remember, it is necessary if one controls these immediate objects, to have other objects or environments in which one does *not* absolutely control. Why is this?

It is because LIFE IS A GAME.

The word "game" is used here advisedly. When one is mired down in the sometimes titanic struggle of existence, he is apt to discount the fact that there is joy in living. He is apt to disbelieve that such a thing as fun can exist. Indeed, people when they reach into their thirties begin to wonder what happened to their childhood, when they actually could enjoy things.

One begins to wonder if "pleasure of living" isn't itself some sort of trap. And one begins to believe that it is not a good thing to become too interested in new people and new things since these will only lead to heartbreak. There are men who have decided that, in view of the fact that loss brings so much pain, they had better not acquire at all. It is far superior, according to these, to live a life of only medium privation than to live a life of considerable luxury—since then, if they lost what they have, the pain would be much less.

Life, however, is a game. It is very easy to see a game in terms of cricket or football. It is not so easy to see life as a game when one is forced to arrive before the sun rises and reaches home only after it sets—after a day of arduous and relatively unthanked toil. One is likely to dispute that such an activity could be a game at all. Nevertheless it is obvious—in various experiments which have been made in Scientology—that life, no matter what its emotional tone or lack of it, is in essence a game. And that the elements of life itself are the elements of games.

ANY JOB IS A GAME.

A game consists of:

FREEDOM, BARRIERS and PURPOSES.

There are many more complicated factors involved in games, but these are all listed in Scientology.

Primary amongst these is the necessity in a game to have an opponent or an enemy. Also a necessity is to have problems. Another necessity is to have sufficient individuality to cope with the situation. To live life fully, then, one must have in addition to "something to do," a higher purpose. And this purpose, to be a purpose at all, must have counter-purposes or purposes which prevent it from occurring. One must have individualities which oppose the purpose or activities of one. And if one lacks these things, it is certain that he will invent them.

"Any job is a game."

This last is very important. If a person lacks problems, opponents and counter-purposes to his own, *he will invent them.* Here we have, in essence, the totality of "aberration." But more intimately to our purposes, we have the difficulties which arise from work.

If we had a foreman who capably controlled everything in his area and did nothing else and if that foreman was not entirely mentally balanced in all ways (which is to say, if he were human), we would find that foreman *inventing* personalities for the workers under him and reasons why they were opposing him and actual oppositions. We would find him selecting out one or more of his workmen to chastise with, according to the foreman, "very good reasons"—but in actuality, without any further reason than that the foreman obsessively needs opponents. Now, very many involved classifications can be read into this by ancient mental analyses. But none of these need to be examined. The truth of the matter is that a man must have a game. And if he does not have one, he will make one. If that man is aberrated and not entirely competent, he will make an intensely aberrated game.

Where an executive finds all running far too smoothly in his immediate vicinity, he is likely to cause some trouble just to have something to do—unless that executive is in very good mental condition indeed. Thus, we have management pretending, often without any actual basis in fact, that labor is against it. Similarly, we occasionally have labor certain that management, which is in fact quite competent, is against labor. Here we have invented a game where no game can actually exist.

When men become very shortsighted, they cannot look, actually, beyond their own environment. There is—in any office, plant or activity—the game of the office, plant or activity itself, versus its competitors and versus its outer environment.

If that office, plant or activity and all the personnel within it are conducting themselves on a wholly rational and effective basis, they choose the outside world and other rival concerns for their game. If they are not up to par and are incapable of seeing the real game, they will make up a game. And the game will begin to be played inside the office and inside the plant.

In playing games, one has individuals and teams. Teams play against teams, individuals play against individuals. When an individual is not permitted to be fully a part of the team, he is apt to choose other members of the team as his opponents. For, remember, Man *must* have a game.

Out of all these complexities come the various complexities of work and the problems of production and communication.

If everybody in a plant were able to control his own sphere of interest in that plant and if everybody in the plant were doing his own job, there would actually be no lack of game. For there are other plants, other activities in the outside world, and these always furnish game enough for any rational organization. But supposing the people in an organization cannot control their own sphere, cannot control their own activities and are obsessively attempting to create aberrated games all about them. Then we would have a condition whereby the plant, office or concern would not be able to effectively fight its environment and would produce poorly, if not collapse.

Aberrated or not aberrated, competent or not competent, remember, life is a game. And the motto of any individual or team alive is:

THERE *MUST* BE A GAME.

If individuals are in good mental and physical condition, they actually play the game which is obvious and in plain sight.

If they are not in good condition and if they are themselves incapable of controlling their own immediate environment, they will begin to play games with their tools.

Here, the machinist will find his machine suddenly incapable of producing. One would not go so far as to say that he will actually break the machine so that he can have a game with it. But he will be in a mild state of fury regarding that machinery continually.

The bookkeeper, unable to control his immediate tools of trade and not well fitted into his concern, will begin to play a game with his own figures and will fail to get balances. His adding machine will break down, his papers will get lost and other things will occur under his immediate nose which never should happen. And if he were in good shape and could play the actual game of keeping other people in the plant straight, so far as their accounts and figures are concerned, he would be efficient.

Efficiency, then, could be defined as "the ability to play the game to hand." Inefficiency could be defined as "an inability to play the game to hand, with a necessity to invent games with things which one should actually be able to control with ease."

This sounds almost too simple but, unfortunately for the professors that try to make things complicated, it is just that simple. Of course, there are a number of ways men can become aberrated. That is not the subject of this book. The subject of this book is work.

Now, realizing that life *must* be a game, one should realize that there is a limit to the area one would control and still retain an interest in life. Interest is mainly kindled by the unpredictable. Control is important. Uncontrol is, if anything, even more important. To actually handle a machine perfectly, one must be *willing* to control it or not to control it.

When control itself becomes obsessive, we begin to find things wrong with it. The individual who absolutely has to control everything in sight is upsetting to all of us. And this individual is why we have begun to find things wrong with control.

It sounds very strange to say that *un*control must also be under control. But this is, in essence, true. One must be *willing* to leave certain parts of the world uncontrolled. If he cannot, he rapidly drops downscale and gets into a situation where he is obsessively attempting to control things which he never will be able to control and, thus, renders himself unhappy, begins to doubt his ability to control those things which he actually should be able to control and so, at length, loses his ability to control anything. And this, in essence, is what we in Scientology call the "dwindling spiral of control."

There are mental factors, which we will not discuss here, which tend to accumulate the failures to control to a point where one is no longer confident of his ability to control. The truth of the matter is an individual actually desires to have some part of life uncontrolled. When this part of life hurts him sufficiently, he then resigns himself to the necessity of controlling it and so makes himself relatively unhappy if he never will be able to do so.

A game consists of freedom, barriers and purposes. It also consists of:

CONTROL and UNCONTROL.

An opponent in a game *must* be an uncontrolled factor. Otherwise, one would know exactly where the game was going and how it would end. And it would not be a game at all. Where one football team would be totally capable of controlling the other football team, we have no football game. This is a matter of "no contest." There would be no joy or sport in playing that game of football.

Now, if a football player has been seriously injured playing football, a new unknowing factor enters into football for *him*. This injury lodges in what we call the "reactive mind." It is a mind which is unseen and which works all the time. One normally works on what we call the "analytical mind" and this we know all about. Anything that we have forgotten, or moments of unconsciousness and pain, become locked away in the reactive mind and are then capable of *reacting* upon the individual in such a way as to make him refrain from doing something which was once dangerous. While this is a rather technical subject, it is nevertheless necessary to understand that one's past has a tendency to accumulate and victimize one in the future. Thus in the case of the football player. While he plays football, he is apt to be *restimulated* or *react from* the old injury received in football and so feels less than a spirit of fun while playing football. He becomes anxious. He becomes very grim on the subject of football. And this is expressed by an effort to actively control the players on another team so that they will not injure him again.

In a motorcycle race, a famous motorcycle rider was injured. Two weeks later, in another race, we find this motorcycle rider falling out on the fifth lap without injury or incident, but simply pulling over into the pits. He did this immediately after a motorcycle swerved close to him. He recognized at once that he was unable to control *that* motorcycle. He felt, then, incapable of controlling his *own* motorcycle and so knew one thing—he had to get out of that race. And just as this motorcycle rider abandoned the race, so all of us at one time or another have abandoned sections of life.

Now, up to the time he had that accident, the motorcycle rider was perfectly unwilling to control any other motorcycle on the track save his own. He did not worry about these other motorcycles since they had never injured him, and the motorcycle racing game was still a game to him. However, during the accident there was a moment when he sought to control another motorcycle than his own and another rider. He failed in that effort. Thus in his "reactive mind" there is an actual "mental image picture" of his failing to control a motorcycle. Thus in future racing he is less competent. He is afraid of his own machine. He has identified his own machine with somebody else's machine. But this is a failure of control.

Now, in order to become a good motorcycle racer again, this man would have to resume his attitude of carelessness regarding the control of the other machines and riders on the track and reassume his own ability to control his own machine. If he were able to do this, he would become once more a daring, efficient and winning motorcycle rider demonstrating great competence. Only a Scientology practitioner could put him back into this condition—and a Scientology practitioner would be able to do this probably in a very few hours.

This, however, is not a textbook on how to eradicate former ills, but an explanation of why men become incompetent in the handling of their immediate tools of trade. These men have attempted to leave uncontrolled all the world around them up to the moment when the world around them *hurt* them. They then conceived the idea that they should control more than their own jobs. They failed to control more than their own jobs and were instantly convinced that they were incapable of controlling something. This is quite different than leaving things uncontrolled. To be capable of controlling things and to be capable of leaving things uncontrolled are both necessary to a good life and doing a good job. To become convinced that one cannot control something is an entirely different thing.

The whole feeling of self-confidence and competence actually derives from one's ability to control *or* leave uncontrolled the various items and people in his surroundings.

When one becomes obsessed with a necessity to control something rather beyond his sphere of control, he is disabused of his ability to control those things close to him. A person eventually gets into a state of mind where he cannot pay any attention at all to his own job, but can only reach out into the outer environment and seek—effectively or otherwise—to stop, start or change things which have, in reality, very little to do with his own job. Here we have the agitator, the inefficient worker, the individual who is going to fail. He is going to fail because he *has* failed at some time in the past.

This is not quite as hopeless as it looks because it takes actual physical injury and very heavy duress to make an individual feel that he is incapable of controlling things. The day-to-day handling of machinery is not what deteriorates one's ability to work or handle life. It is not true that one gets old and tired and his ability to do things "wears out." It *is* true that one becomes injured in sudden, short moments and thereafter carries that injury into his future work and the *injury* is what causes him to deteriorate. The eradication of the injury brings him back to an ability to control his own environment.

The entire subject of work, then, brings us to the value of *uncontrol.*

A machinist doing a good job should be able to relax as far as his machine is concerned. He should be able to let it run or not let it run, to start it or not to start it, to stop it or not to stop it. If he can do these things, all with confidence and a calm state of mind, he can then handle that machine and it will be discovered that the machine will run well for him. Now, let us say the machine "bites him"—he hurts his hand in it, some other worker jostles against him at the wrong moment, some tool given to him is defective and shatters. An actual physical pain enters into the situation. He tends to fall away from the machine. He tends, then, to concentrate much more heavily on the machine than he should. He is no longer willing to leave it uncontrolled. When he is working with that machine, he *must control it*. Now, as he has entered duress into this situation and as he is already anxious about it, it is fairly certain that the machine will hurt him again. This gives him a second injury. And with this injury, he feels an even stronger urge to control the machine.

You see, during the moments of injury the machine was out of control. Now, while "out of control" is a game condition, it is not desired or welcome to this particular machinist. Eventually, it is very certain, he will look upon this machine as some sort of a demon. He will, you might say, run the machine all day and at night, while asleep, run it too. He will spend his weekends and his holidays still "running" that machine. Eventually, he will not be able to stand the sight of that machine and will flinch at the idea of working it a moment longer. This picture becomes slightly complicated by the fact that it is not always the injury delivered to him by his own particular machine which causes him to feel anxious about machinery. A man who has been in an automobile accident may return to the working of a machine with considerable qualms about machines in general. He begins to identify his *own* machine with *other* machines and *all* machines become the *same* machine and that is *the* machine that hurt him!

There are other conditions which enter into lighter phases of work.

In the matter of a clerk, we may have a circumstance where he is ill from some other area than his area of work and yet, because he has little time off, is forced to work sick or not. The tools of his own work—his filing cabinets or his pens or books or the very room—become identified with his feeling of sickness and he feels that these, too, have "bitten him." Thus, he becomes obsessed in his control of them and actually degenerates in his ability to control them, just as the machinist does.

Even though these tools have not actually injured him, he associates them with "being injured." In other words, he identifies his own sickness with the work he is doing.

Thus even a clerk—whose tools of trade are not particularly dangerous—can become upset about his tools of trade and can, first, exert *enormous* control over them on an obsessed basis and, at length, abandon *any* control of them and feel he would rather be beaten than do an instant's more work in his particular sphere.

One of the ways of getting over such a condition is to simply *touch* or handle one's various tools of the trade and the surroundings in which he works. If a man were to go all the way around an office in which he had worked for years and touch the walls and window ledges and the equipment and tables and desks and chairs—ascertaining carefully the feel of each one, carefully locating each one with regard to the walls and other items in the room—he would feel much better about the entire room. He would be, in essence, moving himself in a moment of time where he was sick or injured, up to present time.

The maxim here is that:

ONE MUST DO ONE'S WORK IN PRESENT TIME.

ONE MUST NOT CONTINUE TO WORK IN OLD MOMENTS OF INJURY.

If acquaintance with one's tools—or touching one's tools of the trade and discovering exactly where and how they are—is so beneficial, then what would be the mechanism behind this?

We will leave until later in this book some drills and exercises calculated to rehabilitate one's ability to work and look for a moment at this new factor.

"If a man were to go all the way around an office in which he had worked for years and touch the walls and window ledges and the equipment and tables and desks and chairs...he would feel much better about the entire room."

CHAPTER SIX

AFFINITY,
REALITY AND
COMMUNICATION

AFFINITY, REALITY AND COMMUNICATION

THERE ARE THREE FACTORS in Scientology which are of the utmost importance in handling life. These three factors answer the questions: How should I talk to people? How can I sell people things? How can I give new ideas to people? How can I find what people are thinking about? How can I handle my work better?

We call this, in Scientology, the A-R-C TRIANGLE.

It is called a triangle because it has three related points.

The first of these points is:

AFFINITY.

The second of these points is:

REALITY.

The third of these points and the most important is:

COMMUNICATION.

These three factors are related.

"We call this, in Scientology, the A-R-C TRIANGLE.
It is called a triangle because it has three related points.
The first of these points is: Affinity. The second of these
points is: Reality. The third of these points and
the most important is: Communication."

By affinity we mean "emotional response." We mean "the feeling of affection or lack of it, of emotion or mis-emotion connected with life."

By reality we mean "the solid objects, the *real* things of life."

By communication we mean "an interchange of ideas between two terminals (people)."

Without affinity, there is no reality or communication. Without reality, there is no affinity or communication. Without communication, there is neither affinity nor reality. Now, these are sweeping statements, but are nevertheless very valuable and are true.

Have you ever tried to talk to an angry man? An angry man's communication is at a level of mis-emotion which repels all terminals from him. Therefore his communication factor is very low, even though very loud. He is attempting to destroy something or some other terminal. Therefore his reality is very poor. Very likely what he is apparently "being angry about" is not what has made him mad. An angry man is not truthful. Thus it could be said that his reality, even on the subject he is attempting to voice, is poor.

There must be good affinity (which is to say, affection) between two people before they are very real to each other (and reality must here be used as a gradient, with things being *more real* than other things). There must be good affinity between two people before they can talk together with any truth or confidence. Before two people can be real to each other, there must be some communication between them. They must at least see each other which is, in itself, a form of communication. Before two people can feel any affinity for each other, they must to some degree be real.

These three terms are interdependent one upon the other. And when one drops, the other two drop also. When one rises, the other two rise also. It is only necessary to improve one corner, of this very valuable triangle in Scientology, in order to improve the remaining two corners. It is only necessary to improve two corners of the triangle to improve the third.

To give you some idea of a practical application of this, there is the case of a young girl who had run away from home and whose parents would no longer talk to her. The girl, as a clerk in an office, was quite despondent and was doing very bad work—at which time this matter became of intense interest to the office manager. Now, ordinarily in the workaday world, the office manager would have dismissed her and found another girl. But employment was critical at the time and this office manager knew the modern thing to do: He sent for a Scientologist.

The Scientologist, whose attention had been directed to her by the office manager, gave her an interview and discovered that her parents were intensely angry with her and would no longer communicate with her at all. They had been so upset at her refusal (actually, her inability) to follow a career as a concert pianist, for which they had her studying at great expense, that they had "washed their hands of her." And the unpleasantness had forced her to run away to a distant point. Since that time, they had not communicated *with* her, but had spoken to people she had known in her home neighborhood, in very bitter terms, *concerning* her. In such a state of mind—since she was intimately involved with her parents and wished to be on the best possible terms with them—she could not work. Her failure to perform her work was jamming communication lines in her own office. In other words, her affinity was very low. And her reality on things was quite low, since she might be said to have been "elsewhere" most of the time. And thus the communication lines which passed through her hands were equally low and successfully jammed other communication lines in the office.

The Scientologist, knowing well this A-R-C Triangle, did a very ordinary thing—to a Scientologist—which apparently worked "magic" as far as the girl was concerned. He told the girl that she must write to her parents and regardless of whether they replied or not, she *must* write. And she did so.

Naturally, there was no reply. Why was there no reply from the parents? Well, the girl, having disobeyed them and having moved out from underneath their control, was apparently no longer in contact with them. These parents did not consider her as *real*. She did not actually *exist* as far as they were concerned. They had actually said this to themselves. They had actually tried to wipe her out of their lives since she was "such a disappointment." Therefore they had no emotion about her whatsoever, except perhaps a sort of *apathy*. They had been unable to control her. And so they were apathetic about her *since* they had failed to control her. At this stage, the parents were glumly apathetic about the girl and she was not very real to them at all. As a matter of fact, to have started her on a career she could not complete, the girl could not have been very real to them in the first place since the career was undoubtedly beyond the girl's capabilities.

So the Scientologist had her write another letter. This letter was, as we say in Scientology, entirely "good roads and good weather." The girl said that she was "working in this other city," that "the weather was good," that she "was getting along well and hoped that they were both well," and sent them her love. The letter carefully did not take up any of the problems or activities immediately behind her leaving home. The A of the letter, the affinity, was quite high. The C was present. What the Scientologist was trying to do was establish R, reality—the reality of the situation of the girl's being in another city and the actual reality of her existence in the world. He knew that she was sufficiently involved with her parents that if *they* did not consider her real, she was not even real to *herself*.

Of course, when the parents did not answer this letter, the Scientologist had the girl write again. And after four letters—all of which more or less said the same thing and entirely ignored the idea that there'd been no reply—there was a sudden letter from the mother to the girl, which was *angry* (not with the girl, but with one of her old playmates). The girl, coached, was "held in line" by the Scientologist. She was not permitted to explode back through the communication line, but was coaxed into writing a "surprised," pleasant letter expressing her happiness at having heard from her mother.

After this, two letters came—one from the father and one from the mother. Both of them were very affectionate and hoped the girl was doing well. The girl, of course, replied to these very joyously, but would have been completely propitiative if the Scientologist had permitted her to do so. Instead, a happy letter went back to each of them.

And in return, two more letters came, both of them very congratulatory to the girl at having found a job and something that she was interested in doing in life and requests as to where her clothes should be sent and, actually, a small draft of money to help her along in the city. The parents had already begun to plan the new career of the girl which was in exact line with what the girl could do in life—stenographic work.

Of course, the Scientologist knew exactly what was going to happen. He knew that *their* affinity and reality would come up. And that the *girl's* reality, affinity and communication, in the office itself, would rise as soon as this situation was remedied. He remedied with communication, expressing affinity from the girl. And this, of course, as it always does, produced reaction. The girl's work came up to par, the girl began to progress and, now that her feeling of reality was sufficiently high, actually became a very valuable office worker.

Probably the reason why the A-R-C Triangle went so long undiscovered was the fact that a person in apathy rises through various "tones." These tones are quite uniform, one follows the next, and people *always* come up through these tones one after the other. These are the tones of affinity. And the Tone Scale of Dianetics and Scientology is probably the best possible way of predicting what is going to happen next or what a person actually will do.

The Tone Scale starts well below apathy. In other words, a person is feeling no emotion about a subject at all. An example of this was the American attitude concerning the atomic bomb. Something about which they should have been very concerned was so far beyond their ability to control and so likely to end their existence that they were *below apathy* about it. They actually did not even feel that it was very much of a problem. Americans "processed" on this particular subject had to be worked with for some little time until they began to feel *apathetic* about the atomic bomb. This was really an advance over the feeling of no emotion whatsoever on a subject which should have intimately concerned them. In other words, on many subjects and problems, people are actually well below apathy.

There, the Tone Scale starts—utter dead, null, far below death itself. Going up into improved tones, one encounters the levels of:

BODY DEATH
APATHY
GRIEF
FEAR
ANGER
ANTAGONISM
BOREDOM
ENTHUSIASM
SERENITY, in that order.

Enthusiasm

Serenity

Antagonism

Boredom

Fear

Anger

Apathy

Grief

THE TONE SCALE

Body Death

There are many small stops between these tones, but one knowing anything about human beings should definitely know these particular emotions.

A person who is in *apathy* when his tone is improved feels *grief.*

A person in *grief* when his tone improves feels *fear.*

A person in *fear* when his tone improves feels *anger.*

A person in *anger* when his tone improves feels *antagonism.*

A person in *antagonism* when his tone improves feels *boredom.*

When a person in *boredom* improves his tone he is *enthusiastic.*

When an *enthusiastic* person improves his tone he feels *serenity.*

Actually, the *below apathy* level is so low as to constitute a no-affinity, no-emotion, no-problem, no-consequence state of mind on things which are actually tremendously important. The area below apathy is an area without pain, interest, beingness or anything else that matters to anyone. But it is an area of grave danger, since one is below the level of being able to respond to anything and may accordingly lose everything without apparently *noticing* it.

A workman who is in very bad condition—and who is actually a liability to the organization—may not be capable of experiencing pain or any emotion on any subject. He is below apathy. We have seen workmen who would hurt their hand and "think nothing of it" and go right on working, even though their hand was very badly injured. People in dispensaries, working in industrial areas, are quite amazed sometimes to discover how little attention some workmen pay to their own injuries. It is an ugly fact that people who pay no attention to their own injuries and who are not even feeling pain from those injuries are not and never will be, without some attention from a Scientologist, efficient people.

They are liabilities to have around. They do not respond properly. If such a person is working a crane and the crane suddenly goes out of control to dump its load on a group of men, that sub-apathy crane operator will simply let the crane drop its load. In other words, he is a potential murderer. He cannot stop anything, he cannot change anything and he cannot start anything. And yet, on some automatic response basis, he manages some of the time to hold down a job. But the moment a real emergency confronts him, he is not likely to respond properly and accidents result.

Where there are accidents in industry, they stem from these people in the sub-apathy tone range. Where bad mistakes are made in offices which cost firms a great deal of money, lost time and cause other personnel difficulties, such mistakes are found rather uniformly to stem from these sub-apathy people. So do not think that one of these states of being unable to feel anything, of being numb, of being incapable of pain or joy is any use to anyone. It is not. A person who is in this condition cannot control things and, in actuality, is not "there" sufficiently to be controlled by anyone else and does strange and unpredictable things.

Just as a person can be chronically in sub-apathy, so a person can be in apathy. This is dangerous enough, but is at least expressed. Only when we get up into apathy itself do we have the A-R-C Triangle beginning to manifest itself and become visible. Communication from the person himself—not from some "circuit" or "training pattern"—is to be expected.

People can be chronically in grief, chronically in fear, chronically in anger or in antagonism or boredom or, actually, can be "stuck in enthusiasm." A person who is truly able is normally fairly serene about things. He can, however, express other emotions and it is a mistake to believe that a total serenity is of any real value. When a situation which demands tears cannot be cried about, one is not in serenity as a chronic tone.

Serenity can be mistaken rather easily for this sub-apathy, but of course only by a very untrained observer. One glance at the physical condition of the person is enough to differentiate: People who are in sub-apathy are normally quite ill.

Just as we have a range of the Tone Scale thus covering the subject of affinity, so do we have one for *communication*. On the level of each of the emotions, we have a communication factor. In sub-apathy, an individual is not really communicating at all. Some social response or training pattern or, as we say, "circuit" is communicating. The person himself does not seem to be there and isn't really talking. Therefore his communications are sometimes strange, to say the least. He does the wrong things at the wrong time. He says the wrong things at the wrong time. Naturally, when a person is "stuck" on any of the bands of the Tone Scale—sub-apathy, apathy, grief, fear, anger, antagonism, boredom, enthusiasm or serenity—he voices communications with that emotional tone. A person who is always angry about something is stuck in anger. Such a person is not as bad off as somebody in sub-apathy, but he is still rather dangerous to have around since he will make trouble. And a person who is angry does not control things well. The communication characteristics of people at these various levels on the Tone Scale are quite fascinating. They say things and handle communication, each in a distinct characteristic fashion for each level of the Tone Scale.

Just as in affinity and communication, there is a level of *reality* for each of the affinity levels. Reality is an intensely interesting subject since it has to do, in the main, with relative *solids.* In other words, the solidity of things and the emotional tone of people have a definite connection. People low on the Tone Scale cannot tolerate solids. They cannot tolerate a solid object. The thing is not real to them. It is thin or lacking in weight. As they come upscale, the same object becomes more and more solid and they can finally see it in its true level of solidity.

93

In other words, these people have a definite reaction to mass at various points on the scale. Things are bright to them or very, very dull. If you could look through the eyes of a person in sub-apathy, you would see a very watery, thin, dreamy, misty, unreal world indeed. If you looked through the eyes of an angry man, you would see a world which was "menacingly" solid, where all the solids posed a "brutality" toward him. But they still would not be sufficiently solid, or sufficiently real or visible, for a person in good condition. A person in serenity can see solids as they are, as bright as they are and can tolerate an enormous heaviness or solidity without reacting to it. In other words, as we go up the Tone Scale from the lowest to the highest, things can get more and more solid and more and more real.

Affinity is most closely related to *space*. In fact, affinity could be defined as the "consideration of distance," since terminals which are far apart or close together have different affinity reactions one to another.

Reality, as we have seen, is most intimately connected with *solids*.

Communication consists of the *flow* of ideas or particles across *space* between *solids*.

While these definitions may seem very elementary and would not at all satisfy an MIT professor, they actually outreach and encompass an MIT professor's whole field of activity. Truths do not have to be complicated.

There are—as described at considerable length and studied with considerable depth in Scientology—many interrelations of spaces, solids and ideas or particles, since these are the most intimate things to livingness itself and comprise the universe around us.

But the most basic thing we should know about A-R-C is simply emotional tone, which is affinity; the actuality of things, which is the reality; and the relative communication ability concerning them.

Men who can do things are very high on affinity, very high in terms of reality and are very capable in terms of communication. (If you wish to measure their various capabilities, you should study the subject much further. A whole book has been written about this triangle, called *Science of Survival*.)

Then, how *would* you talk to a man?

You cannot talk adequately to a man if you are in a sub-apathy condition. In fact, you would not talk to him at all. You would have to have a little higher affinity than that to discuss things with anyone. Your ability to talk to any given man has to do with your emotional response to any given man. Anyone has different emotional responses to different people around them. In view of the fact that two terminals (that is to say, two *people*) are always involved in communication, one could see that someone else would have to be somewhat real. If one does not care about other people at all, one will have a great deal of difficulty talking to them—that is certain. The way to talk to a man, then, would be to find something to like about him and to discuss something with which he can agree. This is the downfall of most new ideas—one does not discuss subjects with which the other person has any point of agreement at all.

And we come to a final factor with regard to reality: That with which we agree tends to be more real than that with which we do not agree. There is a definite coordination between agreement and reality. Those things are real which we agree are real. Those things are not real which we agree are not real. On those things with which we disagree, we have very little reality.

An experiment based on this would be an even jocular discussion between two men of a third man who is present. Two men agree on something with which the third man cannot agree. The third man will drop in emotional tone and will actually become less real to the two people who are discussing him.

How *do* you talk to a man, then?

You establish reality by finding something with which you both agree. Then you attempt to maintain as high an affinity level as possible by knowing there is something you can like about him. And you are then able to talk with him. If you do not have the first two conditions, it is fairly certain that the third condition will not be present (which is to say, you will not be able to talk to him easily).

You should realize in using the A-R-C Triangle that, once more, the emotional tones are progressed through as one begins to develop communication. In other words, somewhere up the line, somebody who has been totally apathetic about us is liable to become angry at us. If one can simply persevere up through this anger, he reaches only antagonism, then boredom and finally enthusiasm and a perfect communication level and understanding.

Marriages fall apart simply because of a failure of communication, because of the failure of reality and affinity. When communication starts failing, the affinity starts dropping, people have secrets from one another and their affinity starts out the bottom.

Similarly, in an office or a business, it is perfectly easy to establish those people who are doing things which are not to the best interests of the firm, since these people go gradually—and sometimes not so gradually—out of communication with the firm. Their emotional tone toward their superiors and those around them starts dropping and finally goes out the bottom.

As can be seen, the A-R-C Triangle is intimately bound up with an ability to control and an ability to leave uncontrolled. When an individual attempts to control something and fails to do so, he then experiences an antipathy toward that thing. In other words, he has not been right. He has been wrong. His intention has failed. His intention has, you might say, backfired upon him. Thus as one attempts to control things and then fails to control them, he is likely to drop down Tone Scale about those things. Thus an individual who has been betrayed by the tools of his own trade is apt to treat them with a lowering affinity level. He becomes bored with them, he becomes antagonistic toward them, he becomes angry with them and, at this stage, the machinery starts to break up. And finally, he becomes afraid of them, becomes sad about them, becomes apathetic about them and no longer cares about them at all and, at this stage, certainly cannot use them at all. Actually, from the level of boredom down, the ability to use one's tools of the trade is consistently lowered.

Now, how could one knowing this raise his ability to control the tools of the trade without even going to a Scientologist? Naturally, if a Scientologist took over in this situation, the entirety of control of tools, or an area, or of life could be regained. But lacking this, how could one simply handle the exact articles with which he is right now and immediately associated?

By using A-R-C he could regain, in some measure, both his control of the tools and his enthusiasm for work. He would do this by communicating and discovering his willingness for these and the people around him to be real or solid.

An individual could regain his ability over his immediate tools simply by *touching them* and *letting them go*. This might seem rather pointless and he is apt to reach the level of boredom and become bored with the process. Just above this level is the pay of becoming enthusiastic.

It sounds very strange that if one simply touched his automobile and let go, and touched it and let go, and touched it and let go, and touched it and let go, possibly for some hours, he would regain not only his enthusiasm for the automobile, but a tremendous ability to control the automobile which he had never suspected in himself at all.

It sounds strange that if we made a bookkeeper pick up and lay down his pencil or pen, for a couple of hours, he would regain his ability to handle it and would improve in his ability to make figures. And if we got him to touch and let go of his ledger, for a considerable length of time, that he would be more capable of handling that ledger and would make far fewer mistakes with it.

Similarly with people, since these often object to being touched, one can communicate. If one really communicates and communicates well to these people—listens to what they have to say and acknowledges what they say and says what he has to say to them, gently enough and often enough so that it is actually received by them—he will regain, to a very marked degree, his ability to associate and coordinate the actions of those people with whom he is immediately surrounded.

Here we have A-R-C immediately adjusted to work.

This sounds like magic. It is magic. It is Scientology.

"If one really communicates and communicates well
to these people... he will regain, to a very marked
degree, his ability to associate and coordinate
the actions of those people with whom
he is immediately surrounded."

CHAPTER SEVEN

EXHAUSTION

EXHAUSTION

To WORK OR NOT TO WORK? That is the question. The answer to that question in most men's minds is EXHAUSTION.

One begins to feel after he has been long on a job, has been considerably abused on that job, that to work any more would be quite beyond his endurance. He is tired. The thought of doing certain things makes him tired. He thinks of raising his energy or of being able to force his way along just a little bit further. And if he does so, he is thinking in the wrong channels, since the answer to exhaustion has little, if anything, to do with energy.

Exhaustion is a very important subject not only to an individual involved in earning his own living, but to the state as well.

Scientology has rather completely established the fact that the downfall of the individual begins when he is no longer able to work. All it is necessary to do to degrade or upset an individual is to prevent him from working. Even the police have now come to recognize the basic Scientology principle that the primary thing wrong with a criminal is that he *cannot work*. And police have begun to look for this factor in an individual in establishing his criminality.

The basic difficulty with all juvenile delinquency is the one-time apparently humane program of forbidding children to labor in any way. Doubtless it was once a fact that child labor was abused, that children were worked too hard, that their growths were stunted and that they were, in general, used. It is highly doubtful if the infamous Mr. Marx ever saw, in America, young boys being pulled off machines, dead from work and thrown onto dump heaps. Where there was an abuse of this matter, there was a public cry against it. And legislation was enacted to prevent children from working.

This legislation, with all the good intention of the world, is, however, directly responsible for juvenile delinquency. Forbidding children to work and, particularly, forbidding teenagers to make their own way in the world and earn their own money, creates a family difficulty so that it becomes almost impossible to raise a family. And it creates, as well and particularly, a state of mind in the teenager that "the world does not want him" and he has already lost his game before he has begun it. Then, with something like Universal Military Training staring him in the face so that he dare not start a career, he is of course thrust into a deep sub-apathy on the subject of work. And when he, at length, is faced with the necessity of making his own way in the world, he rises into an apathy and does nothing about it at all.

It is highly supportive of this fact that our greatest citizens worked, usually, when they were quite young. In the Anglo-American civilization, the highest level of endeavor was achieved by boys who from the age of twelve, on farms, had their own duties and had a definite place in the world.

Children, in the main, are quite willing to work. A two-, three-, four-year-old child is usually to be found haunting his father, or her mother, trying to help out either with tools or dust rags. And the kind parent, who is really fond of the children, responds in the reasonable and long-ago normal manner of being patient enough to let the child actually assist. A child, so permitted, then develops the idea that his presence and activity are desired and he quite calmly sets about a career of accomplishment. The child who is warped or pressed into some career, but is not permitted to assist in those early years, is convinced that he is not wanted and that the world has no part of him. And later on, he will come into very definite difficulties regarding work.

However, the child who at three or four wants to work— in this modern society—is discouraged and is actually prevented from working. And after he is made to be idle until seven, eight or nine, is suddenly saddled with certain chores. Now, this child is already educated into the fact that he "must not work." And so the idea of work is a sphere where he "knows he does not belong" and so always feels uncomfortable in performing various activities. Later on, in his teens, he is actively prevented from getting the sort of a job which will permit him to buy the clothes and treats for his friends which he feels are demanded of him. And so he begins to feel he is not part of the society. Not being part of the society, he is then against the society and desires nothing but destructive activities.

The subject of exhaustion is also the subject of "prevented work." In the case of soldiers and sailors hospitalized during any one of these recent wars, it is found that a few months in a hospital tends to break the morale of the soldier or sailor to such a point that he may become a questionable asset when returned to his service. This is not necessarily the result of his lowered abilities. It is the result of injury compounded by inactivity. A soldier who is wounded and cared for in a field hospital close to "the front," and is returned to duty the moment he can possibly support such duties, will be found to retain, in a large measure, his morale. Of course, the injury received has a tendency to repel him from the level of action which he once thought best.

But even so, he is in better shape than a soldier who is sent to a hospital in "the rear." The soldier who is sent to the hospital in the rear is being told, according to his viewpoint, that he is not particularly necessary to the war.

Without actually adding up these principles, the word "exhaustion" began a general use coupled with "neurosis." Now, this was based on the fact that people with a neurosis simply looked exhausted. There was no more coordination to it than that. Actually, a person who has been denied the right to work, particularly one who has been injured and then denied the right to work, will eventually encounter exhaustion.

Technically, in Scientology, it is discovered that there is no such thing as a "gradual diminishing, by continuing contact, of the energy of the individual." One does not become exhausted simply because one has worked too long or too hard. One becomes exhausted when he has worked sufficiently long to restimulate some old injury. One of the characteristics of this injury will be "exhaustion." Chronic exhaustion, then, is not the product of long hours and arduous application. It is the product of the accumulation of the shocks and injuries incident to life, each of them perhaps only a few seconds or a few hours long and adding up perhaps to a totality of only fifty or seventy-five hours. But this accumulation—the accumulation of injury, repulsion and shock—eventually mounts up to a complete inability to do anything.

Exhaustion can, then, be trained into a person by refusing to allow him as a child to have any part of the society. Or it can be beaten into a person by the various injuries or shocks he may receive incident to his particular activity. Clear up either of these two points and you have cleared up exhaustion. Exhaustion, then, is actually the subject of a Scientology practitioner—since only a Scientologist can adequately handle it.

There is a point, however, which is below exhaustion. This is the point of not knowing when one is tired. An individual can become a sort of hectic puppet that goes on working and working and working, without even realizing that he is working at all, and suddenly collapsing from a tiredness he was not experiencing. This is our sub-apathy Tone Scale again.

And again we have the subject of control. Here, the individual has failed to control things, has tried and has then gone down Tone Scale about them into the sub-apathy band. Eventually, he is incapable of handling anything even resembling tools of the trade or an environment of work and so is unable to inhabit such an environment or handle such tools. The individual can then have many hard words cast in his direction. He can be called "lazy," he can be called "a bum," he can be called "criminal." But the truth of the matter is, he is no more capable of righting his own condition—without expert help—than he is capable of diving to the center of the Earth.

There are some means of recovering one's verve and enthusiasm for work, short of close work with a Scientology practitioner. These are relatively simple and very easy to understand.

We have, in Scientology, something we call INTROVERSION.

And, something else we call EXTROVERSION.

Introversion is a simple thing. It means "looking in too closely."

And extroversion is also a simple thing. It means nothing more than "being able to look outward."

It could be said that there are "introverted personalities" and "extroverted personalities." An extroverted personality is one who is capable of looking around the environment. An introverted personality is only capable of looking inward at himself.

"It could be said that there are 'introverted personalities' and 'extroverted personalities.'"

When we examine the A-R-C Tone Scale, we see at once that an introverted personality is shying away from solids. In other words, he is not confronting reality. Reality is *agreement* in the mental plane and is *solids* in the physical plane.

A person who is capable of looking at the world around him and seeing it quite real and quite bright is, of course, in a state of extroversion. In other words, he can "look out." He can also work. He can also see situations and handle and control those things which he *has* to handle and control and can stand by and watch those things which he does *not* have to control and be interested in them, therefore.

The person who is introverted is a person who has probably passed exhaustion some way back. He has had his attention focused closer and closer to him (basically, by old injuries which are still capable of exerting their influence upon him) until he is actually looking inward and not outward. He is shying away from solid objects. He does not see a reality in other people and things around him.

Now let us take the actual subject of work.

Work is "the application of attention and action to people or objects located in space."

When one is no longer able to confront people or objects or the space in which they are located, he begins to have a "lost" feeling. He begins to move in a mistiness. Things are not real to him and he is relatively incapable of controlling those things around him. He has accidents, he has bad luck, he has things turn against him simply because he is not handling them or controlling them or even observing them correctly. The future to him seems very bad, so bad sometimes that he cannot face it. This person could be said to be severely introverted.

In work, his attention is riveted on objects which are usually, at the most, only a few feet from him. He pays his closest attention to articles which are within the reach of his hands. This puts his attention away from extroversion, at least to some spot of focus in front of his face. His attention fixes there. If this is coincident with some old injury, incident or operation, he is likely to fix his attention as well on some spot in former times and become *restimulated*—so that he gets the pains and ills and the feeling of tiredness or apathy or sub-apathy which he had during that moment of injury. As his attention is continuously riveted there, he of course has a tendency to look *only* there even when he is not working.

Let us take an accountant. An accountant's eyes are on books at fixed distances from his eyes. At length, he becomes "shortsighted." Actually, he doesn't become shortsighted, he becomes "book-sighted." His eyes most easily fix on a certain point in distance. Now, as he fixes his attention *there,* he tends to withdraw even from *that* point until, at length, he does not quite reach even his own books. Then, he is fitted with glasses so that he can see the books more clearly. His vision and his attention are much the same thing.

A person who has a machine or books or objects continually at a fixed distance from him, leaves his work and tends to keep his attention fixed exactly where his work was. In other words, his attention never really leaves his work at all. Although he goes home, he is still really "sitting in the office." His attention is still fixed on the environment of his work. If this environment is coincident with some injury or accident (and who does not have one of these, at least?) he begins to feel weariness or tiredness.

Is there a cure for this? Of course, only a Scientology practitioner could clear up this difficulty entirely. But the worker does have something which he can do.

Now, here is the *wrong* thing to do, regardless of whether one is a bookkeeper, an accountant, a clerk, an executive or a machinist. The wrong thing to do is to leave work, go home, sit down and fix attention on an object more or less at the same distance from one as one confronts continually at work.

In the case of a foreman, for instance, who is continually talking to men at a certain distance away from him, the wrong thing for him to do is to go home and talk to his wife at the same distance. The next thing she knows, she will be getting orders just as though she were a member of the shop!

Definitely the wrong thing to do is to go home and sit down and read a paper, eat some dinner and go to bed. If a man practiced the routine of working all day and then sitting down "to rest" with a book or a newspaper in the evening, it is certain that, sooner or later, he would start to feel quite exhausted. And then, after a while, would fall even below that and would not even wonder at his unwillingness to perform tasks which were once very easy to him.

Is there a *right* thing to do? Yes, there is. An individual who is continually fixed upon some object of work should fix his attention otherwise *after* working hours.

Now, here is a process known as:

TAKE A WALK.

This process is very easy to perform.

When one feels tired on finishing his work—no matter if the thought of doing so is almost all that he can tolerate without falling through the floor—he should go out and *walk around the block* until he feels rested. In short, he should walk around the block and *look* at things until he *sees* the things he is walking near. It does not matter how many times he walks around the block, he should walk around the block until he feels better.

In doing this, it will be found that one will become a little brighter at first and then will become very much more tired. He will become sufficiently tired that he "knows" now that he should go to bed and have a good night's sleep. This is *not* the time to stop walking, since he is walking through exhaustion. He is "walking out" his exhaustion. He is not handling the exhaustion by physical exercise. The physical exercise has always appeared to be the more important factor to people, but the exercise is relatively unimportant. The factor that is important is the unfixing of his attention from his work to the material world in which he is living.

Masses are reality. To increase one's affinity and communication, it is actually necessary to be able to confront and tolerate masses. Therefore, walking around the block and looking at buildings will be found to bring one upscale. When one is so tired that he can barely drag himself around, or is so tired that he is hectically unable to rest at all, it is actually necessary that he confront masses. He is simply low on the Tone Scale. It is even doubtful if there is such a thing as a "fall of physical energy." Naturally, there is a limit to this process. One cannot work all day and walk around the block all night and go to work the next day again and still expect to feel relieved. But one should certainly spend some time extroverting after having introverted all day.

Take a Walk is, within reason, a near cure-all.

If one feels antagonistic towards one's wife, the wrong thing to do is to "beat her"! The right thing to do is to go out and take a walk around the block until one feels better and make her walk around the block in the opposite direction until an extroversion from the situation is achieved—since it will be discovered that all domestic quarrels, particularly amongst working people, stem from the fact of having been overfixed (rather than overstrained) on their work and the situations connected with it. One has failed to control certain things in his working environment. He then comes home and seeks to find something he *can* control. This is usually the marital partner or the children. And when one fails even there, he is apt to drop downscale with a vengeance.

The extroversion of attention is as necessary as the work itself. There is nothing really wrong with introverting attention or with work. If one didn't have something to be interested in, he would go to pieces entirely. But if one works, it will be found that an unnatural tiredness is apt to set in. When this is found to be the case, then the answer is not a "drop into unconsciousness" for a few hours—as in sleep—but in actually extroverting the attention and then getting a *really* relaxing sleep.

These principles of introversion and extroversion have many ramifications. And although Take a Walk is almost laughable in its simplicity, there are many more complicated processes in case one wishes to get more complicated. However, in the main, Take a Walk will take care of an enormous number of difficulties attendant to work.

Remember that, when doing it, one will get more tired at first and will then get fresher. This phenomenon has been noted by athletes. It is called the "second wind." The second wind is really getting enough environment and enough mass in order to "run out" the exhaustion of the last race. There is no such thing as a second wind. There is such a thing as a return to extroversion on the physical world in which one lives.

Similar to Take a Walk is another process known as:

LOOK THEM OVER.

If one has been talking to people all day, has been selling people all day or has been handling people who are difficult to handle all day, the *wrong* thing to do is to run away from all the people there are in the world.

You see, the person who gets overstrained when handling people has had large difficulties *with* people. He has perhaps been operated upon by doctors and the half-seen vision of them standing around the operating table identifies "all people" with "doctors" (that is to say, all people who stand still). This, by the way, is one of the reasons why doctors become so thoroughly hated in a society—since they do insist on practices known as surgery and anesthesia and such incidents become interlocked with everyday incidents.

Exhaustion because of contact with people actually indicates that the "havingness" (another Scientology term for "reality") of people has been reduced. One's attention has been fixated upon certain people while his attention, he felt, ought to be on other people. And this straining of attention has actually cut down the number of people that he was observing. Fixed attention, then, upon a few people can actually limit the number of people one can "have" (which is to say, limit one's reality on people in general).

The cure for this is a very simple one. One should go to a place that is very well populated—such as a railroad station or a main street—and should simply walk along the street noting people. Simply *look at people,* that is all. It will be found, after a while, that one feels people "aren't so bad" and one has a much kinder attitude toward them. But, more importantly, the job condition of becoming overstrained with people tends to go away if one makes a practice of doing this every late afternoon for a few weeks.

This is one of the smartest things that a salesman can do, since a salesman, above and beyond others, has a vested interest in being able to handle people and get them to do exactly what he wants them to do (which is to say, buy what he has to sell). As he fixes his attention on just one too many customers, he gets tired of the whole idea of talking to people or selling and goes down Tone Scale in all of his activities and operations, begins to consider himself all kinds of a "swindler" and, at length, doesn't consider himself anything at all. He, like the others, should simply find populated places and walk along looking at people. He will find, after a while, that people really do exist and that they aren't so bad.

One of the things that happens to people high in government is that they are being continually "protected from" the people. And they, at length, become quite disgusted with the whole subject and are apt to do all manner of strange things. (See the lives of Hitler and Napoleon.)

This principle of introversion and extroversion could go much further in a society than it does. There is something that could be done—by the government and by businesses in general—which would probably eradicate the idea of strikes and would increase production quite markedly. Workers who strike are usually discontented not so much with the "conditions of work," but with work itself. They feel they are being victimized. They are being pressed into working at times when they do not want to work. And a strike comes as an actual relief. They can fight something. They can do something else than stand there and fiddle with a piece of machinery or account books. Dissatisfied workers are striking workers. If people become exhausted at work, if people are not content with work, if people are upset with work, they can be counted upon to find a sufficient number of grievances to strike. And if management is given enough trouble and lack of cooperation on the part of the people on the lower chains of command, it can be certain that management, sooner or later, will create situations which cause workers to strike. In other words, bad conditions of work are actually not the reason for labor troubles and disputes. Weariness of work itself, or an inability to control the area and environments of work, *are* the actual cause of labor difficulties.

Any management given sufficient income to do so, if that management is not terribly aberrated, will pay a decent working wage. And any workman given a half-chance will perform their duties cheerfully. But once the environment itself becomes overstrained, once the company itself has become introverted by "overt acts" on the part of the government, once the workers have been shown that they have no control over management—there can be, after that, labor disputes. Underlying all these obvious principles, however, are the principles of introversion and extroversion. Workers become so introverted at their task that they no longer are capable of affinity for their leaders and are no longer capable, actually, of viewing the environment in which they work. Therefore, someone can come along and tell them that "all the executives are ogres," which is obviously not true. And on the executive level, someone can come along and tell the executives that "all the workers are ogres," which is obviously, on that side, not true either.

In the absence of broad treatment on individuals, which is a gargantuan task, a full program could be worked out that would handle the principle of introversion. It is certain that if workers or managers get introverted enough, they will then find ways and means of inventing aberrated games—such as strikes—and so disrupt production and decent relationships and living conditions within the factory, the office or the concern.

The cure would be to extrovert workers on a very broad scale. This could be done, as one solution, by making it possible for all workers to have two jobs. It would be necessary for the company or related interests—such as the government—to actually make available a sufficient number of "public works projects" to provide work for workers outside the sphere of exact application. In other words, a man who is made to work continually *inside* and at a very fixed task, would find a considerable relief at being able to go *outside* and work—particularly at some *disrelated* task.

As an example, it would be a considerable relief to an accountant to be able to dig ditches for a while. A machinist, running a stationary machine, would actually find it a very joyful experience to push around a bulldozer.

Such a plan, then, would actually take *introversion* and *extroversion* with a large hand and bring it about. Workers who are working in fixed positions, with their attention very close to them, would then be permitted to look more widely and to handle things which tended to extrovert them. Such a program would be very ambitious. But it would be found, it is certain, to result in better labor-management relations, better production and a considerable lessening of working and public tension on the subjects of jobs and pay.

In short, there are many things that could be done with the basic principle of introversion-extroversion.

The principle is very simple. When an individual is made too introverted, things become less real in his surroundings, and he has less affinity for them and cannot communicate with them well. Furthermore, what *does* communicate is apt to communicate at his lowered Tone Scale so that even good news will be received poorly by him. In such a condition, he becomes tired easily. Introversion results in weariness, exhaustion and then an inability to work. The remedy for it is extroversion—a good look at and communication with the wider environment. And unless this is practiced, then in view of the fact that any worker is subject to injuries or illnesses of one kind or another, a dwindling spiral will ensue which makes work less and less palatable until, at length, it cannot be performed at all. And we have the basis of not only a nonproductive, but a criminal society.

CHAPTER EIGHT

THE MAN WHO
SUCCEEDS

THE MAN WHO SUCCEEDS

THE CONDITIONS OF SUCCESS are few and easily stated.

Jobs are not held, consistently and in actuality, by flukes of fate or fortune. Those who depend upon luck generally experience bad luck.

The ability to hold a job depends, in the main, upon ability. One must be able to control his work and must be able to be controlled in doing his work. One must be able, as well, to leave certain areas uncontrolled. One's intelligence is directly related to his ability. There is no such thing as being too smart. But there is such a thing as being too stupid.

But one may be both able and intelligent without succeeding. A vital part of success is the ability to handle and control not only one's tools of the trade, but the people with whom one is surrounded. In order to do this, one must be capable of a very high level of affinity, he must be able to tolerate massive realities and he must, as well, be able to give and receive communication.

The ingredients of success are then, first, an ability to confront work with joy and not horror, a wish to do work for its own sake, not because one "has to have a paycheck." One must be able to work without driving oneself or experiencing deep depths of exhaustion. If one experiences these things, there is something wrong with him. There is some element in his environment that he should be controlling that he isn't controlling. Or his accumulated injuries are such as to make him shy away from all people and masses with whom he should be in intimate contact.

The ingredients of successful work are training and experience in the subject being addressed, good general intelligence and ability, a capability of high affinity, a tolerance of reality and the ability to communicate and receive ideas.

Given these things, there is left only a slim chance of failure. Given these things, a man can ignore all of the accidents of birth, marriage or fortune—for birth, marriage and fortune are not capable of placing these necessary ingredients in one's hands.

One could have all the money in the world and yet be unable to perform an hour's honest labor. Such a man would be a miserably unhappy one.

The person who studiously avoids work usually works far longer and far harder than the man who pleasantly confronts it and does it. Men who cannot work are not happy men.

Work is the stable datum of this society. Without something to do, there is nothing for which to live. A man who cannot work is as good as dead and usually prefers death and works to achieve it.

The mysteries of life are not today, with Scientology, very mysterious. Mystery is not a needful ingredient. Only the very aberrated man desires to have vast secrets held away from him.

Scientology has slashed through many of the complexities which have been erected for men and has bared the core of these problems. Scientology, for the first time in Man's history, can predictably raise intelligence, increase ability, bring about a return to the ability to play a game and permits Man to escape from the dwindling spiral of his own disabilities. Therefore work itself can become, again, a pleasant and happy thing.

There is one thing that has been learned in Scientology, which is very important to the state of mind of the workman. One very often feels, in his society, that he is working for the immediate paycheck and that he does not gain, for the whole society, anything of any importance. He does not know several things. One of these is how *few* good workmen are. On the level of executives, it is interesting to note how precious any large company finds a man who can handle and control jobs and men *really* is. Such people are rare. All the empty space in the structure of this workaday world is at the top.

And there is another thing which is quite important. And that is the fact that the world today has been led to believe—by mental philosophies calculated to betray it—that when one is dead, it is all over and done with and one has no further responsibility for anything. It is highly doubtful if this is true. One inherits tomorrow what he died out of yesterday.

Another thing we know is that men are not dispensable. It is a mechanism of old philosophies to tell men that "If they think they are indispensable, they should go down to the graveyard and take a look—those men were indispensable too." This is the sheerest foolishness. If you really looked carefully in the graveyard, you would find the machinist who set the models going in yesteryear and without whom there would be no industry today. It is doubtful if such a feat is being performed just now.

A workman is not just a workman. A laborer is not just a laborer. An office worker is not just an office worker. They are living, breathing, important pillars on which the entire structure of our civilization is erected. They are not cogs in a mighty machine. They are the machine itself.

We have come to a low level of the ability to work. Offices depend very often on no more than one or two men and the additional staffs seem to add only complexity to the activities of the scene. Countries move forward on the production of just a few factories. It is as though the world were being held together by a handful of desperate men who, by working themselves to death, may keep the rest of the world going.

But again, they may not.

It is to them that this book is dedicated.

*"It is as though the world were being
held together by a handful of desperate men
who, by working themselves to death,
may keep the rest of the world going.
But again, they may not.
It is to them that this book is dedicated."*

APPENDIX

FURTHER STUDY
BOOKS & LECTURES BY L. RON HUBBARD

The materials of Dianetics and Scientology comprise the largest body of information ever assembled on the mind, spirit and life, rigorously refined and codified by L. Ron Hubbard through five decades of research, investigation and development. The results of that work are contained in hundreds of books and more than 3,000 recorded lectures. A full listing and description of them all can be obtained from any Scientology Church or Publications Organization. (See *Guide to the Materials* at page 136.)

Dianetics is a forerunner and substudy of Scientology. On the following pages are the recommended books and lectures for beginners. They appear in the sequence Ron wrote or delivered them. Not the least advantage of a chronological study of these books and lectures is the inclusion of words and terms which, when originally used, were defined by LRH with considerable exactitude. Through a sequential study, you can see how the subject progressed and not only obtain greater comprehension, but application to your life.

The listing of books and lectures below shows where *The Problems of Work* fits within the developmental line. From there you can determine your *next* step or any earlier books and lectures you may have missed. You will then be able to fill in missing gaps, not only gaining knowledge of each breakthrough, but greater understanding of what you've already studied.

Your next book is *Scientology: The Fundamentals of Thought*.

This is the path to *knowing how to know*, unlocking the gates to a better future for *you*. Travel it and see.

DIANETICS BOOKS
AND LECTURES

DIANETICS: THE ORIGINAL THESIS • Ron's *first* description of Dianetics. Originally circulated in manuscript form, it was soon copied and passed from hand to hand. Ensuing word of mouth created such demand for more information, Ron concluded the only way to answer the inquiries was with a book. That book was Dianetics: The Modern Science of Mental Health, now the all-time self-help bestseller. Find out what started it all. For here is the bedrock foundation of Dianetic discoveries: the *Original Axioms,* the *Dynamic Principle of Existence,* the *Anatomy of the Analytical* and *Reactive Mind,* the *Dynamics,* the *Tone Scale,* the *Auditor's Code* and the first description of a *Clear.* Even more than that, here are the primary laws describing *how* and *why* auditing works. It's only here in Dianetics: The Original Thesis.

DIANETICS: THE EVOLUTION OF A SCIENCE • This is the story of *how* Ron discovered the reactive mind and developed the procedures to get rid of it. Originally written for a national magazine—published to coincide with the release of Dianetics: The Modern Science of Mental Health—it started a wildfire movement virtually overnight upon that book's publication. Here then are both the fundamentals of Dianetics as well as the only account of Ron's two-decade journey of discovery and how he applied a scientific methodology to unravel the mysteries and problems of the human mind. And, hence, the culmination of Man's 10,000-year search.

DIANETICS: THE MODERN SCIENCE OF MENTAL HEALTH • The bolt from the blue that began a worldwide movement. For here is Ron's landmark book presenting his discovery of the *reactive mind* that underlies and enslaves Man. It's the source of nightmares, unreasonable fears, upsets and insecurity. And here is the way to get rid of it and achieve the long sought goal of Clear. This is the complete handbook of Dianetics procedure and, with it any two reasonably intelligent people can break the chains that have held them prisoner to the upsets and trauma of the past. A bestseller for more than half a century and with tens of millions of copies in print, translated in more than fifty languages and used in more than 100 countries of Earth, *Dianetics* is indisputably the most widely read and influential book about the human mind ever written. And for that reason, it will forever be known as *Book One.*

DIANETICS LECTURES AND DEMONSTRATIONS • Immediately following the publication of *Dianetics,* LRH began lecturing to packed auditoriums across America. Although addressing thousands at a time, demand continued to grow. To meet that demand, his presentation in Oakland, California, was recorded. In these four lectures, Ron related the events that sparked his investigation and his personal journey to his groundbreaking discoveries. He followed it all with a personal demonstration of Dianetics auditing—the only such demonstration of Book One available, and invaluable to the Dianeticist. *4 lectures.*

SELF PROCESSING

SELF ANALYSIS—*THE BASIC SELF-PROCESSING HANDBOOK* • The barriers of life are really just shadows. Learn to know yourself—not just a shadow of yourself. Containing the most complete description of consciousness, Self Analysis takes you through your past, through your potentials, your life. First, with a series of self-examinations and using the Hubbard Chart of Human Evaluation, you plot yourself on the Tone Scale. Then, applying a series of light yet powerful processes, you embark on the great adventure of self-discovery. This book further contains embracive principles that reach *any* case, from the lowest to the highest—including auditing techniques so effective they are referred to by Ron again and again through all following years of research into the highest states. In sum, this book not only moves one up the Tone Scale but can pull a person out of almost anything.

HANDBOOK FOR PRECLEARS—*THE ADVANCED SELF-PROCESSING HANDBOOK* • Here are the Fifteen Acts of Self-processing oriented to the rehabilitation of *Self-determinism.* Moreover, this book contains several essays giving the most expansive description of the *Ideal State of Man.* Discover why behavior patterns become so solidly fixed; why habits seemingly can't be broken; how decisions long ago have more power over a person than his decisions today; and why a person keeps past negative experiences in the present. It's all clearly laid out on the Chart of Attitudes—a milestone breakthrough that complements the Hubbard Chart of Human Evaluation—plotting the ideal state of being and one's *attitudes* and *reactions* to life. *In self-processing, Handbook for Preclears is used in conjunction with Self Analysis.*

SCIENTOLOGY BOOKS

THEORY AND PRACTICE

SCIENTOLOGY: THE FUNDAMENTALS OF THOUGHT—*THE BASIC BOOK OF THE THEORY AND PRACTICE OF SCIENTOLOGY FOR BEGINNERS* • Designated by Ron as the *Book One of Scientology*. After having fully unified and codified the subjects of Dianetics and Scientology came the refinement of their *fundamentals*. Originally published as a résumé of Scientology for use in translations into non-English tongues, this book is of inestimable value to both the beginner and advanced student of the mind, spirit and life. Equipped with this book alone, one can begin a practice and perform seeming miracle changes in the states of well-being, ability and intelligence of people. Contained within are the *Cycle-of-Action, Conditions of Existence, Eight Dynamics, ARC Triangle, Parts of Man,* the full analysis of *Life as a Game,* and more, including exact processes for individual application of these principles in processing. Here, then, in one book, are the very fundamentals of Scientology for application across one's entire life and the means to uplift the entire culture.

WORK

THE PROBLEMS OF WORK—*SCIENTOLOGY APPLIED TO THE WORKADAY WORLD* • *(This current volume.)* As Ron describes in this book, life is composed of seven-tenths work, one-tenth familial, one-tenth political and one-tenth relaxation. Here, then, is Scientology applied to that seven-tenths of existence including the answers to *Exhaustion* and the *Secret of Efficiency.* Here, too, is the analysis of life itself—a game composed of exact rules. Know them and you succeed. Problems of Work contains technology no one can live without, and that can immediately be applied by anyone in the workaday world.

LIFE PRINCIPLES

SCIENTOLOGY: A NEW SLANT ON LIFE • Scientology essentials for every aspect of life. Basic answers that put you in charge of your existence, truths to consult again and again: *Is It Possible to Be Happy?, Two Rules for Happy Living, Personal Integrity, The Anti-Social Personality* and many more. In every part of this book you will find Scientology truths that describe conditions in *your* life and *exact* ways to improve them.

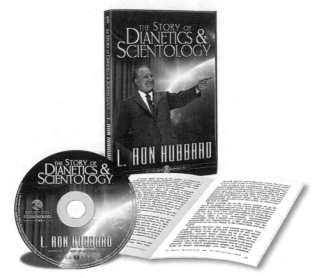

AND YOU CAN *MEET* L. RON HUBBARD

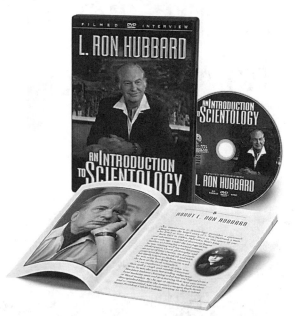

IN HIS *ONLY* FILMED INTERVIEW

What is Scientology?

What is the practical application of Scientology for the average man in the street?

How can Scientology help people overcome their problems?

Why is Man on this planet and what is his purpose here?

Such are the questions posed by millions and, in this rare filmed interview, Ron provided the answers: what *drove* his quest to help Mankind, his hard won *discoveries* providing the long sought answers to the riddles of the mind and life, and how he forged a *route* to accomplish new states of beingness and happiness—here it is as Ron himself explained it to the world.

Meet the man who founded a new religion in the atomic age, a religion that now spans the globe, a religion changing the face of Earth, a religion where science and religion finally meet and so … a religion that could only have been called *Scientology.*

Get

An Introduction to Scientology

GET YOUR FREE

GUIDE TO THE

MATERIALS

- All books
- All lectures
- All reference books

All of it laid out in chronological sequence with descriptions of what each contains.

YOU'RE ON AN ADVENTURE! HERE'S THE MAP.

Your journey to a full understanding of Dianetics and Scientology is the greatest adventure of all. But you need a map that shows you where you are and where you are going.

That map is the Materials Guide Chart. It shows all Ron's books and lectures with a full description of their content and subject matter so you can find exactly what *you* are looking for and precisely what *you* need.

New editions of all books include extensive glossaries, containing definitions for every technical term. And as a result of a monumental restoration program, the entire library of Ron's lectures are being made available on compact disc, with complete transcripts, glossaries, lecture graphs, diagrams and issues he refers to in the lectures. As a result, you get *all* the data and can learn with ease, not only gaining a full *conceptual* understanding, but each step of the way ascending to higher states of personal freedom.

To obtain your FREE Materials Guide Chart and Catalog, or to order L. Ron Hubbard's books and lectures, contact:

WESTERN HEMISPHERE:
Bridge Publications, Inc.
4751 Fountain Avenue
Los Angeles, CA 90029 USA
www.bridgepub.com
Phone: 1-800-722-1733
Fax: 1-323-953-3328

EASTERN HEMISPHERE:
New Era Publications International ApS
Store Kongensgade 53
1264 Copenhagen K, Denmark
www.newerapublications.com
Phone: (45) 33 73 66 66
Fax: (45) 33 73 66 33

Books and lectures are also available direct from Churches of Scientology.
*See **Addresses**.*

ADDRESSES

Scientology is the fastest-growing religion in the world today. Churches and Missions exist in cities throughout the world, and new ones are continually forming.

To obtain more information or to locate the Church nearest you, visit the Scientology website:

www.scientology.org

e-mail: info@scientology.org

or

Phone: 1-800-334-LIFE

(for US and Canada)

You can also write to any one of the Continental Organizations, listed on the following page, who can direct you to one of the thousands of Churches and Missions world over.

L. Ron Hubbard's books and lectures may be obtained from any of these addresses or direct from the publishers on the previous page.

CONTINENTAL CHURCH ORGANIZATIONS:

UNITED STATES

CHURCH OF SCIENTOLOGY
CONTINENTAL LIAISON OFFICE
WESTERN UNITED STATES
1308 L. Ron Hubbard Way
Los Angeles, California 90027 USA
info@wus.scientology.org

CHURCH OF SCIENTOLOGY
CONTINENTAL LIAISON OFFICE
EASTERN UNITED STATES
349 W. 48th Street
New York, New York 10036 USA
info@eus.scientology.org

CANADA

CHURCH OF SCIENTOLOGY
CONTINENTAL LIAISON OFFICE
CANADA
696 Yonge Street, 2nd Floor
Toronto, Ontario
Canada M4Y 2A7
info@scientology.ca

LATIN AMERICA

CHURCH OF SCIENTOLOGY
CONTINENTAL LIAISON OFFICE
LATIN AMERICA
Federacion Mexicana de Dianetica
Calle Puebla #31
Colonia Roma, Mexico D.F.
C.P. 06700, Mexico
info@scientology.org.mx

UNITED KINGDOM

CHURCH OF SCIENTOLOGY
CONTINENTAL LIAISON OFFICE
UNITED KINGDOM
Saint Hill Manor
East Grinstead, West Sussex
England, RH19 4JY
info@scientology.org.uk

AFRICA

CHURCH OF SCIENTOLOGY
CONTINENTAL LIAISON OFFICE AFRICA
5 Cynthia Street
Kensington
Johannesburg 2094, South Africa
info@scientology.org.za

AUSTRALIA, NEW ZEALAND & OCEANIA

CHURCH OF SCIENTOLOGY
CONTINENTAL LIAISON OFFICE ANZO
20 Dorahy Street
Dundas, New South Wales 2117
Australia
info@scientology.org.au

**Church of Scientology
Liaison Office of Taiwan**
1st, No. 231, Cisian 2nd Road
Kaoshiung City
Taiwan, ROC
info@scientology.org.tw

EUROPE

CHURCH OF SCIENTOLOGY
CONTINENTAL LIAISON OFFICE EUROPE
Store Kongensgade 55
1264 Copenhagen K, Denmark
info@scientology.org.dk

**Church of Scientology
Liaison Office of Commonwealth
of Independent States**
Management Center of Dianetics
and Scientology Dissemination
Pervomajskaya Street, House 1A
Korpus Grazhdanskoy Oboroni
Losino-Petrovsky Town
141150 Moscow, Russia
info@scientology.ru

**Church of Scientology
Liaison Office of Central Europe**
1082 Leonardo da Vinci u. 8-14
Budapest, Hungary
info@scientology.hu

**Church of Scientology
Liaison Office of Iberia**
C/Miguel Menendez Boneta, 18
28460 – Los Molinos
Madrid, Spain
info@spain.scientology.org

**Church of Scientology
Liaison Office of Italy**
Via Cadorna, 61
20090 Vimodrone
Milan, Italy
info@scientology.it

GET A FREE
SIX-MONTH MEMBERSHIP
IN THE INTERNATIONAL
ASSOCIATION OF SCIENTOLOGISTS

The International Association of Scientologists is the membership organization of all Scientologists united in the most vital crusade on Earth.

A free Six-Month Introductory Membership is extended to anyone who has not held a membership with the Association before.

As a member, you are eligible for discounts on Scientology materials offered only to IAS Members. You also receive the Association magazine, *IMPACT,* issued six times a year, full of Scientology news from around the world.

The purpose of the IAS is:

"To unite, advance, support and protect Scientology and Scientologists in all parts of the world so us to achieve the Aims of Scientology as originated by L. Ron Hubbard."

Join the strongest force for positive change on the planet today, opening the lives of millions to the greater truth embodied in Scientology.

**JOIN THE INTERNATIONAL
ASSOCIATION OF SCIENTOLOGISTS.**

To apply for membership,
write to the International
Association of Scientologists
c/o Saint Hill Manor, East Grinstead
West Sussex, England, RH19 4JY
www.iasmembership.org

EDITOR'S GLOSSARY
OF WORDS, TERMS AND PHRASES

Words often have several meanings. The definitions used here only give the meaning that the word has as it is used in this book. Dianetics and Scientology terms appear in bold type. Beside each definition you will find the page on which it first appears, so you can refer back to the text if you wish.

This glossary is not meant to take the place of standard language or Dianetics and Scientology dictionaries, which should be referred to for any words, terms or phrases that do not appear below.

—The Editors

aberrated: affected by *aberration*. Aberrated conduct would be wrong conduct, or conduct not supported by reason. Aberration is a departure from rational thought or behavior; not sane. *See also* **aberration**. Page 70.

aberration: departure from rational thought or behavior; not sane. From the Latin, *aberrare,* to wander from; Latin, *ab,* away, *errare,* to wander. It means basically to err, to make mistakes, or more specifically to have fixed ideas which are not true. The entire cause of aberration is contained in the discovery of the previously unknown *reactive mind.* Its entire anatomy, and the eradication of its harmful effects (that cause aberration), are contained in the book *Dianetics: The Modern Science of Mental Health.* Page 70.

absorption: a state or condition of involving the complete attention of or wholly occupying the activities of. Page 7.

abused: 1. hurt or injured by mistreatment. Page 103.
2. used wrongly or improperly; misused. Page 104.

accident: a circumstance produced by chance that is fortunate or lucky, as in *"the accident of what one is born."* Page 5.

143

accidentals: things, events, situations, occurring unexpectedly, unintentionally or by chance. Page 7.

according to (one's) lights: as one's opinions, information or standards may direct. Page 59.

accumulate: gather or pile up, often in gradual degrees. Page 73.

adept: very skilled; expert. Page 52.

advisedly: after careful or thorough consideration; deliberately. Page 67.

agitate: to stir up feeling, interest and support through speeches and writing in something such as a cause. Page 45.

agitator: a person who tries to stir up people in support of a social or political cause, often used in an unfavorable sense. Page 76.

all manner of: all sorts of. Page 8.

all thumbs: lacking physical coordination, skill or grace; clumsy or awkward, as if one's hands contained all thumbs and no fingers. Page 6.

analytical mind: the analytical mind is the conscious, aware mind which thinks, observes data, remembers it and resolves problems. It would be essentially the conscious mind as opposed to the unconscious mind. In Dianetics and Scientology, the analytical mind is the one which is alert and aware and the reactive mind simply reacts without analysis. Page 74.

anatomy: structure or the arrangement of the parts of something. Page 21.

Ancients, the: the civilized peoples, nations or cultures of ancient times. Page 48.

anesthesia: total or partial loss of sensation, especially tactile sensibility, induced by an anesthetic, an agent that causes loss of sensation with or without the loss of consciousness. Page 114.

Anglo-American: relating to both England and America. Page 104.

antipathetic: hostile or antagonistic; characterized by ill will; opposed in nature or character. Page 46.

antipathy: a feeling of disgust toward something usually together with an intense desire to avoid or turn from it. Page 97.

antiquated: no longer used or useful; obsolete, old-fashioned, out-of-date, etc. Page 56.

apathy: a complete lack of emotion for or interest in things generally; an inability to respond emotionally. An individual in apathy has no energy. Page 20.

aplenty: in large amounts; in abundance. Page 37.

apt: inclined; disposed to; given to; likely. Page 67.

aptitude: a natural ability for something, as for learning; capability; intelligence. Page 5.

arduous: 1. difficult to do; demanding great effort or labor. Page 35. 2. characteristic of a heavy demand; hard to endure and straining; severe. Page 57.

ascertaining: finding out or learning with certainty, especially by examination or investigation. Page 78.

Asia: largest continent, situated in the Eastern Hemisphere, bounded by the Arctic, Pacific and Indian Oceans, and separated from Europe by the Ural Mountains. It includes, in addition to the nations on the land mass, Japan, the Philippines, Taiwan, Malaysia and Indonesia. Page 14.

aspirant: a person who seeks or hopes to attain something, as one who eagerly desires a career, advancement, etc. Page 22.

asserted: put forward by confident and forceful behavior. Page 53.

assuredly: for certain, without a doubt. Page 29.

at length: after some time; in the end; eventually. Page 73.

at once: 1. at the same time; simultaneously. Page 21. 2. immediately; straightaway without any delay. Page 28.

attendant: occurring along with something, or resulting or following from it. Page 113.

attributable: regarded as caused by or as resulting from. Page 52.

attributes: qualities, features or characteristics of somebody. Page 26.

automation: the technique, method or system of operating or controlling equipment and machines by highly automatic means, as by electronic devices, reducing human intervention to a minimum. Page 35.

awry: away from the appropriate, planned or expected course. Page 6.

axioms: statements of natural laws on the order of those of the physical sciences. Page v.

backfired: had the opposite effect to what was expected. Page 97.

bad off: in a bad or poor condition or circumstance. Page 93.

balk: block or halt the occurrence or performance of something. Page 62.

bared: exposed to view; revealed. Page 123.

bear: to accept or have as an obligation, with the sense of having to endure something difficult or painful. Page 8.

bearing: relevant relationship or interconnection (usually followed by *on*). Page 7.

beheld: seen or observed. Page 7.

beingness: the condition of being is defined as the result of having assumed an identity. For example, one's own name, one's own profession, one's physical characteristics. Each or all of these things could be called one's beingness. Beingness is assumed by oneself, or given to one's self, or is attained. Page 91.

bitten: figuratively, hurt or injured; caused a bad or unpleasant effect upon. Page 77.

board: abbreviation for *board of directors*, an official group of persons who direct or supervise some activity; the group of people who are responsible for controlling and organizing a company or organization. Page 5.

born: brought into existence; created. Page 10.

borne: endured or tolerated. Page 20.

botch: a job that has been badly done; an unskilled piece of work; mess. Page 22.

bottom, out the: referring to some condition or state being worse than the lowest level; downward from the bottom. Page 96.

bound up in (with): figuratively, closely related or associated; inseparably connected. From the literal meaning of something being tied together in the same bundle. Page 34.

braked: slowed or stopped as if by a brake applied to a wheel. Page 6.

breaks: chances, opportunities; pieces of good luck; advantages. Page 10.

bring (something) about: to accomplish or cause something; make something happen. Page 117.

bum: a lazy person who avoids work and who seeks to live solely by the support of others. Page 107.

burned: consumed rapidly. Page 7.

byword: a word, phrase or idea expressing the guiding principles or rules of action of a person, group or time period. Page 33.

cabal: a small group of people involved in a secret plan, as against a person or government, especially to obtain economic or political power. Also the secret plots and schemes of such a group. Page 8.

capital: wealth in whatever form, used or capable of being used to produce more wealth. Page 10.

carelessness: lack of concern about something. Page 75.

cast: literally, to throw something (especially something light in weight). Hence, turn or direct toward someone or something. Page 107.

cast out: to force to get out or go away; eject. Page 34.

chain of command: a series of executive positions or of officers and subordinates in order of authority especially with respect to the passing on of orders, responsibility, reports, or requests from higher to lower or lower to higher. Page 60.

chanciness: uncertainty or unpredictability. Page 15.

chaos: a state of utter confusion or disorder; a total lack of organization or order. Also, formless matter such as that might exist before order is put into the physical universe. Page 7.

chap: a fellow; man or boy. Page 6.

charm: a power of pleasing or attracting, as through personality or beauty. Page 5.

chastise: to criticize or condemn severely. Page 70.

child labor laws: a reference to laws passed beginning in the 1830s restricting the employment of children and young teenagers until they have reached a specified age. Page 34.

chronic: that lasts a long time or is continuing. Page 92.

chronically: in a manner that lasts a long time or being of long duration or being in a continuing state. Page 92.

circuit: in electricity, a complete route traveled by an electrical current and which carries out specific actions. In Scientology, the term is used to describe something in the mind acting as a circuit does, performing various functions, especially independently of the person's own volition. Page 92.

close work: carrying out a task, series of steps, etc., in a tight working relationship. Page 107.

clutching: seizing with or as with the hands. Hence, gripping or holding tightly or firmly to something, such as a belief, idea, concept, etc. Page 27.

coast: to act or move along aimlessly or with very little effort. Page 34.

coaxed: persuaded gently to do something. Page 88.

cog(s): 1. a *cog* is literally part of a cogwheel, a wheel that has teeth (called cogs) of hardwood or metal made to insert between the teeth of another wheel so that they mesh. When one cogwheel is rotated, the other wheel is turned as well, thus transferring the motion to drive machinery. Used figuratively. Page 8.

2. See definition 1 above. The term *cog* can be used derogatorily to describe an individual worker (a cog) as carrying out minor, automatic actions as part of a larger, uncaring "machine." This view of the working man as nothing but a "laborer" controlled by larger forces was popularized by Karl Marx in the late 1800s. Marx viewed the worker not as a creative, living individual but as merely part of a mass or class of similar "laborers" tediously carrying out their tasks. *See also* **Marx.** Page 124.

cogwheels: wheels that have teeth (called cogs) of hardwood or metal inserted between the teeth of another wheel so that they mesh. When one cogwheel is rotated, the other wheel is turned as well, thus transferring the motion to drive machinery. Used figuratively to describe an individual worker as carrying out a minor function in relationship to the bigger whole of industry or business. Page 7.

command chart: a graphic display of the jobs or positions in an organization, with the highest position in terms of authority and responsibility at the top and the lowest at the bottom. Page 55.

common denominator: something common to or characteristic of a number of people, things, situations, etc.; shared characteristic. Page 26.

communication line(s): the route along which a communication (particle, message, etc.) travels from one person to another. Page 46.

compass(es): literally, a device for finding directions, usually with a magnetized needle that automatically points to the north. Hence, figuratively something that helps one find the correct course of action. Page 11.

compounded: increased, added to or intensified. Page 105.

concern(s): a commercial or manufacturing company or establishment. Page 71.

condemnation: the act of fixing the punishment or destiny of. Page 5.

condemned: strongly disapproved of. Page 7.

considerable: large in amount, extent or degree. Page 50.

consists: is made up, formed or composed of. Page 47.

constancy: freedom from unpredictable variation; stability. Page 10.

contagious: spreading or tending to spread from one person to another, likened to a disease that is transmitted by direct or indirect bodily contact. Page 61.

convulsion: a period of violent social or political stress, strain and confusion; violent turmoil. Page 10.

correspondence course: an educational course in which the teaching organization, school or institution sends lessons and tests to students by mail, usually at their home. Students return completed work in the same way for grading. Page 8.

countenance: to give or express approval to; permit or tolerate. Page 46.

covert: concealed or hidden; disguised. Page 46.

crane: a large machine used to lift and move heavy objects by means of a hook attached to cables suspended from a supporting, usually movable, beam. Page 92.

creatingness: the condition, state or activity of bringing things into existence. Page 37.

credit: belief; mental acceptance of something. Page 6.

cricket: a bat and ball game popular in a number of countries including England, India and Australia. It is played by two opposing teams of eleven players who try to score runs by hitting a small leather ball with a flat wooden bat, and running between two sets of small wooden posts. Page 68.

cross-purposes: conflicting or contrary purposes, aims or goals. Page 41.

currents: course of events; constant or frequent change of forces. Page 20.

cut: reduced, diminished. Page 10.

cut down: to reduce or diminish to what is conceived of as a proper level of importance, stature, etc.; lessen, decrease. Page 40.

cynical: characteristic of a person who holds a low opinion of humanity; distrustful of human sincerity or integrity. Page 5.

daily grind: a reference to (repetitive) daily work conceived of as dull, difficult and tiring. Page 35.

datum: a single piece of information, as a fact; something known or assumed. Page 22.

daubed: coated with something that soils or stains. Page 6.

degenerates: falls or declines below a normal or desirable level in physical or mental qualities; deteriorates. Page 77.

degree: an academic title given by a college or university to a student who has completed a course of study. Page 6.

delusion: a persistent false belief or opinion that is resistant to reason and confrontation with actual fact. Page 5.

depression: any period marked by slackening of business activity, increased unemployment, falling prices and wages, etc. Page 19.

Depression: a drastic decline in the world economy starting in the United States, resulting in mass unemployment and widespread poverty that lasted from 1929 until 1939. Page 39.

deranged: disturbed the order or arrangement of; upset the normal condition or function of. Page 19.

desperate: facing the worst with firmness of mind or purpose; making a final, ultimate effort; giving all. Page 124.

despondent: in low spirits from loss of hope or confidence. Page 86.

despotic: of or relating to rule with absolute or unlimited powers especially when applied in an unjustly cruel or harsh manner. Page 10.

151

determinism: power of choice or decision. Page 59.

detest: to dislike intensely; hate. Page 39.

Dickens: Charles Dickens (1812–1870), popular English author who wrote about nineteenth-century society and whose stories often depicted eccentric characters. *See also* **"waiting for something to turn up."** Page 21.

diminishing: becoming smaller or less; reducing or decreasing in amount (gradually). *See also* **gradual diminishing by continuing contact.** Page 106.

disabused (of): persuaded or made to believe that an idea or concept is not valid or true. Page 76.

disheartening: that deprives or destroys the enthusiasm, courage, or resolution of someone. Page 10.

dispensable: able to be replaced or done without. Page 123.

dispensary(ies): an office in a hospital, school, workplace or other institution from which medical supplies, preparations and treatments are dispensed. Page 91.

displacing: taking the place of (sometimes by force). Page 10.

do: to serve or be satisfactory; be enough, sufficient or adequate. Page 10.

doctrine: something that is taught or laid down as true concerning a particular subject or department of knowledge. Page 22.

dominance: highest or superior position of influence or control. Page 5.

doubtless: without doubt; certainly. Page 104.

dowager: a woman who holds some title, property or money from her deceased husband. Page 33.

down pat: mastered or learned perfectly. Page 25.

downscale: lower on the Tone Scale. Page 73.

draft: a written order issued by one person, bank, company, etc., directing the payment of money to another; a check. Page 88.

dramatize: imitate, express or act out something, as an actor would in a drama or play acting out his scripted part. Page 40.

driving: compelling or forcing to work, often excessively. Page 122.

drudgery: exhausting, boring or unpleasant work. Page 10.

drunk deep (of): taken in a large amount as if by drinking. Page 40.

ducks: lowers quickly, especially so as to avoid something, such as in lowering the head in a fight to avoid a punch from one's opponent. Used figuratively. Page 20.

dump: having to do with a place where rubbish or garbage is dumped. Page 104.

duress: compulsion by threat or force (of hardship). Page 33.

dwindle: become steadily less; diminish in amount. Page 53.

dwindling spiral: the worse an individual gets, the more capacity he has to get worse. *Spiral* here refers to a progressive downward movement, marking a relentlessly deteriorating state of affairs, and considered to take the form of a spiral. The term comes from aviation where it is used to describe the phenomenon of a plane descending and spiraling in smaller and smaller circles, as in an accident or feat of expert flying, which if not handled can result in loss of control and a crash. Page 73.

dynasties: a series or succession of rulers of the same family or line. Page 10.

Eastern Europe: the part of Europe that includes areas and countries from the eastern part of Germany to the western part of Russia. Page 14.

economy: careful avoidance of financial waste. Page 19.

edge: an improved position; an advantage. Page 8.

effecting: bringing about, accomplishing or making happen. Page 50.

elders: persons greater than another in age or seniority; also, those senior to others in experience. Page 6.

endeavor: purposeful or industrious activity. Page 104.

envision: to have a mental image especially in advance of something. Page 27.

eradication: the action of doing away with something not wanted; a complete removal of something. Page 76.

exact sciences: sciences (such as mathematics or physics), in which facts can be accurately observed and results can be accurately predicted. Page v.

executive secretary: a secretary with independent administrative responsibilities who assists an executive in a business firm. Such responsibilities include the keeping of official corporation records, planning conferences, etc. Page 6.

factor: a circumstance, fact or influence that contributes to a condition, situation or result. Page 6.

fallacy: a false or mistaken idea, opinion, etc.; an error. Page 12.

fault to find: criticism; expressed dissatisfaction. Page 35.

feat: an act or accomplishment showing unusual skill, imagination, etc. Page 123.

fiddle: to play with (using the fingers) as if in an aimless way. Page 25.

firm: company, business or organization. From the Latin *firmus,* meaning secure, the word then meant to ratify by signature, and later commercial house. Page 5.

fitted: adapted, made suitable; had the requirements of. Page 72.

flattened: ruined financially. Page 36.

flinch: to draw back, as from a blow, difficulty, etc. Page 77.

floor, falling through the: falling down in a state of exhaustion, as if with so much impact one drops down through the floor. Page 111.

fluke(s): an accidental advantage or result of an action; chance happening. Page 121.

flung: thrown, especially with great violence or force. Used figuratively. Page 25.

foes: opponents or enemies of somebody or something. Page 20.

folly: inability or refusal to accept existing reality or foresee consequences; a lack of sense or rational conduct; foolishness. Page 33.

forbiddings: things that hinder or prevent or discourage someone from doing something; rules or laws against something. Page 40.

foreman: a person who is in charge of a group of other workers, for example, on a construction site or in a factory. Page 5.

formidable: difficult to deal with; requiring great skill to overcome; challenging. Page 24.

fortune: 1. a supposed power thought of as bringing good or bad to people; chance, regarded as affecting human activities. Page 121.
2. great financial wealth or material possessions. Page 122.

founded: laid the base of or supported, such as a conclusion, with evidence or reasoning. From Latin *fundus* "bottom, base." Page 20.

front: 1. an appearance, usually assumed or pretended, of social standing, wealth, etc. From the specialized meaning of *front*, face or expression of the face indicating state of mind. Page 6.
2. the foremost line or part of an armed force; the furthest position that an army has reached. Page 105.

fumble: to mishandle; to handle inefficiently or unskillfully; make a mess of. Page 35.

gargantuan: of tremendous size or volume. From a story by French writer François Rabelais about Gargantua, a giant noted for his size and huge appetite. Page 116.

gauge: to evaluate, judge or measure somebody or something. Page 60.

gauged: calculated or determined. Page 7.

glumly: in a way or manner that is moody, melancholy and gloomy; quietly miserable. Page 87.

good roads and good weather: characteristic of things, activities or subjects of which everyone is in favor. Page 87.

gradient: a gradual increase or decrease; a little bit more, added to a little bit more, until there is a whole range from a small amount to a large amount, or something goes from a large amount, by gradients, gradually, step-by-step, down into a little bit of something. Page 85.

gradual diminishing by continuing contact: a reference to energy being gradually lessened, as when a battery is in *contact* with an electrical device and is drained by continual use. Page 106.

grave: causing, involving or arising from a threat of danger, harm or other bad consequences. Page 91.

grievances: actual or supposed circumstances regarded as just cause for protest. Page 115.

grimly: in a manner that is firm and determined. Page 29.

grind: something that is routine, dull and tedious, such as work. Page 20.

gritting one's teeth: summoning up one's strength to face unpleasantness or overcome a difficulty. *Grit* is used here in the sense of both clamping one's teeth together and grinding them with effort. Page 21.

half-chance: some opportunity of being or doing something. Page 116.

hand, to: nearby or close; in plain sight or obvious. Page 72.

hand, with a large: from the phrase *helping hand* which means to give aid or assistance to someone. Hence, *with a large hand* is assistance of great quantity affecting many. Page 117.

hard-beaten: struck or pressed by frequent foot traffic; trodden; worn hard, bare or plain by repeated passage. Used figuratively. Page 7.

hard words: (of speech) that which is rude and offensive or criticizes rudely (and unfairly). Page 107.

has no part of (him): *part* means a portion, division, piece or segment of a whole. Hence, the phrase *has no part of (him)* means has nothing to do with (him), has no part or concern in (him). Page 105.

haunting: visiting often or continually; frequenting. Page 104.

heap(s): a pile, mass or mound of things thrown on top of each other. Page 104.

hectic: characterized by intense activity, confusion or haste. Page 107.

held in line: held firm in alignment with some procedure; prevented (someone) from straying off a standard of behavior or action. *Line* means a general method, manner or course of procedure. Page 88.

Hitler: Adolf Hitler (1889–1945), German political leader of the twentieth century who dreamed of creating a master race that would rule for a thousand years as the third German empire. Taking over rule of Germany by force in 1933 as a dictator, he began World War II (1939–1945), subjecting much of Europe to his domination and murdering millions of Jews, others considered "inferior" and even his own people. He committed suicide in 1945 when Germany's defeat was imminent. Page 115.

Homer in the Lotus Isles: a reference to a story from the epic poem *Odyssey,* written by ancient Greek poet Homer (ca. ninth century B.C.). During a ten-year-long voyage on his way home from war, the hero Odysseus and his men are driven ashore by a storm and land upon the island of Lotus-Eaters (natives who feed on the fruit of the legendary lotus plant–referred to in Greek mythology as yielding a fruit that induces blissful forgetfulness and dreamy contentment in those who eat it). After eating from the plant the idle and sluggish crew loses all desire to return to their native land, and have to be dragged back to their ship and tied to their rowing benches. Page 36.

host: a large number; a great quantity. Page 33.

identified: associated or linked one thing with another in the mind, so as to consider or regard them as being one and the same, when in fact they are not identical. This type of irrational thinking was discovered to be the way the reactive mind operates; everything is identified with everything, that is, everything equals everything equals everything. See the book *Dianetics: The Modern Science of Mental Health.* Page 75.

ideology: the doctrines, opinions or way of thinking of an individual, class, etc.; specifically, the body of ideas on which a particular political, economic or social system is based. Page 20.

illusion: a perception that represents what is perceived in a way different from the way it is in reality. Page 5.

incident (to): accompanying something or occurring as a result of it. Page 106.

indispensable: essential, that cannot be gotten rid of or done away with. Page 123.

individuality: the sum of the characteristics or qualities that sets one person apart from others; individual character. Page 68.

Industrial Age: the period in British history from the middle of the eighteenth century to the middle of the nineteenth century characterized by social and economic changes marking the transition from a stable agricultural society to a modern industrial society and relying on complex machinery and large-scale factory production rather than hand tools and home-based manufacturing. By extension, any such period in a country's history. Page 11.

industrialist: one owning or engaged in the management of an especially large-scale industry. Page 20.

industry: 1. energetic application and devotion of oneself to a task or work. Page 5.
2. economic activity concerned with the processing of raw materials and manufacture of goods in factories. Page 92.

inexplicably: in a way that cannot be explained, understood or accounted for. Page 19.

infamous: well known for some bad quality or deed. Page 104.

injunctions: orders from a court or other authority prohibiting or requiring a specific action. Page 34.

in some measure: to a certain extent; in some degree; somewhat. Page 97.

inspiration: a stimulation or animating external influence on the mind (and emotions) that prompts one (creatively) to think a certain way, take action, etc. Used here humorously. Page 27.

intricacies: complicated details or elements. Page 53.

jamming: blocking or obstructing as if by crowding. Page 86.

Jim-Jambo Company: a made-up name for a company. Page 6.

jocular: joking, humorous. Page 96.

jostles: comes in rough contact with while moving; bumps and pushes. Page 76.

juvenile delinquency: antisocial or illegal behavior by young people. Page 104.

kindled: excited, inspired (a passion or feeling); stirred up. Page 72.

labor: 1. productive activity, especially for the sake of economic gain. Page 34.
2. physical or mental work. Page 36.
3. the workers, especially manual workers, in a company, considered as a group. Page 45.

lap: one complete trip around a racetrack, such as in a car or on a horse. Page 74.

large hand, with a: from the phrase *helping hand* which means to give aid or assistance to someone. Hence, *with a large hand* is assistance of great quantity affecting many. Page 117.

legislation: a proposed or enacted law or group of laws. Page 104.

Life: all existence, transcending day-to-day living; the principle or state of conscious spiritual existence; animating force or influence, the cause of living that is the source of vital energy, happiness, etc.; a spiritual form of eternal existence transcending physical death. Page 1.

lights, according to (one's): as one's opinions, information or standards may direct. Page 59.

line: a course of progress or movement; a direction or route. Page 54.

lineage: direct descent from an ancestor; ancestry. Page 5.

lingered: remained or stayed on in a place longer than is usual or expected, as if from reluctance to leave. Page 6.

livingness: the quality or state of living. Page 12.

lodges: becomes fixed, embedded or caught in a place or position; comes to rest. Page 74.

lost to: to have passed from the possession of. Page 61.

lot: one's fortune in life; fate. Page 8.

Lotus Isles: a fabled land described in the poem *Odyssey* by Homer, Greek poet of the ninth century B.C. *See also* **Homer in the Lotus Isles.** Page 36.

machine age: an era which began in the late eighteenth century, notable for its extensive use of mechanical devices, replacing human labor and homemade goods. Page 39.

mad: mentally disturbed; insane. Page 12.

made: brought into existence; created. Page 34.

magnitude: greatness in size, extent, influence, importance, quality, etc. Page 59.

main, in the: for the most part; mainly. Page 45.

Man: the human race or species; humankind; Mankind. Page 1.

man: **1.** a human being, without regard to sex or age; a person. Page 6. **2.** a husband, male lover or sweetheart, as in *"whose total interest was a man or 'stamps.'"* Page 7.

manifest: show plainly; make evident or clear. Page 56.

margin: an amount over and above what is strictly necessary, included, for example, for safety reasons or to allow for mistakes, delays or other unforeseen circumstances. Page 20.

markedly: noticeably, to a significant extent. Page 115.

Marx: Karl Marx (1818–1883), German political philosopher whose works formed the basis of twentieth-century communism and who viewed society as a conflict between the capitalists (factory owners) and the workers. Marx and his fellow communists accused the capitalists of miserable working conditions such as poorly paying the workers, of long hours under unhealthy and dangerous conditions and of abusive child labor. Page 104.

maxim: a statement of a general rule or truth. Page 63.

measures: procedures; courses of action or plans (to achieve a particular purpose); also, laws or proposed laws. Page 45.

menaces: things threatening danger, harm, injury, etc. Page 20.

mental image picture: a picture which, stored in the reactive mind, is a complete recording, down to the last accurate detail, of every perception present in a moment of pain and partial or full unconsciousness. These mental image pictures have their own force and are capable of commanding the body. Page 75.

mired: involved in a difficult situation or condition that is hard to escape from; entangled. Literally, a *mire* is wet, slimy soil of some depth or deep mud. Page 67.

mis-emotion: *mis-* abbreviation of miserable, misery. *Mis-emotion* is anything that is unpleasant emotion such as antagonism, anger, fear, grief, apathy or a death feeling. Page 85.

misnomer: a wrong name; an incorrect designation or term. Page 47.

MIT: Massachusetts Institute of Technology, a technological and scientific institution of higher learning and research located in Cambridge, Massachusetts, USA. Page 94.

Napoleon: Napoleon Bonaparte (1769–1821), French military leader. He rose to power in France by military force, declared himself emperor and conducted campaigns of conquest across Europe until his final defeat by armies allied against him in 1815. Half a million men died in the Napoleonic Wars of 1799–1815. Page 58.

national: of or pertaining to *nationalism,* or a supporter of *nationalism,* the policy or doctrine of asserting the interest of one's own nation, viewed as separate from the interest of other nations or the common interests of all nations. *Nationalism* is often associated with the belief that one country is superior to all others. Page 57.

naught: nothing; be without result. Page 7.

navigating: planning, recording and controlling the course and position of (a ship or an aircraft). Hence, following a planned course on, across or through. Page 19.

not-knowingness: the state or condition of not knowing, being unsure or uncertain. The suffix *-ness* is used when forming nouns expressing a state, quality or condition. Page 12.

notoriously: known widely and usually unfavorably. Page 35.

nullify: to deprive of value or effectiveness. Page 28.

occasion: bring about; cause. Page 57.

ogres: persons who seem fierce and cruel. The word comes from a fairy tale where a giant monster (ogre) eats humans. Page 116.

-ologies: branches of learning. The suffix *-ology* is placed at the end of a word and means "study of" or "knowledge," usually in reference to any science or branch of knowledge; for example, biology (study of living organisms) or geology (study of the physical history of Earth). In the text, it is referring to Freudian psych*ology* and the theory that Man's difficulties are largely caused and motivated by repressed or hidden sexual desires, childhood passions or attractions for the parent of the opposite sex, hostility for the parent of the same sex, etc. Page 11.

outraged: offended greatly against certain standards of how something should be done; angered or shocked. Page 7.

out the bottom: referring to some condition or state being worse than the lowest level; downward from the bottom. Page 96.

overt acts: harmful acts performed against another or others (such as unfair laws, taxes, etc., affecting a business). Page 116.

palatable: acceptable or agreeable to the mind or feelings. Page 117.

par, up to: reaching or operating at the normal state, condition or degree. Page 71.

parade: a succession, sequence or series (of things); from the usual meaning, a large public procession usually including a marching band and often of a festive nature, held in honor of an anniversary, person, event, etc. Page 7.

particles: (small) pieces of something; parts, portions or divisions of a whole. Page 22.

particular: an individual fact or item. Page 24.

pat, down: mastered or learned perfectly. Page 25.

pay: reward or benefit in return for doing something. Page 97.

pension: a sum of money paid regularly as a retirement benefit for past services to an employer. Page 19.

percentile: a percentage; a portion or share in relation to a whole. Page 34.

perpetrated: committed, performed or executed. Page 10.

phenomenon: an observable fact or event. Page 113.

philosophy: a set of opinions, ideas or principles; a basic theory; a view or outlook, as those belonging to a particular field as in political philosophy. Page 21.

pined: had an intense longing or desire for. Page 34.

pits: an area off the side of a racetrack for servicing racing cars or motorcycles during a race. Page 74.

place: position or standing, especially in degree of importance; relative position of merit in any context. Page 6.

plane: a level of existence or thought. Page 109.

plant: a building or group of buildings for the manufacture of a product; a factory. Also the equipment, including machinery, tools, instruments and fixtures, and the buildings containing them, necessary for an industrial or manufacturing operation. Page 20.

plea: earnest and sometimes emotional request. Page 33.

police state: a country in which the government uses police, especially secret police, to exercise strict control over the economic and social life of the people and severely limits their freedom to meet, write or speak about politics. Page 58.

politically: of, relating to or dealing with the responsibilities and duties of government, a body of people or individuals governing the internal and external affairs of a state, nation, etc. Page 34.

post: a position, job or duty to which a person is assigned or appointed. Page 6.

potent: influential; strong; powerful. Page 21.

powers that be: those in command; the authorities. Page 35.

practitioner: a person engaged in the practice of a profession, occupation, etc. Page 75.

present time: now; the current time or moment. Page 78.

president, a great: reference to Franklin Delano Roosevelt (1882-1945), thirty-second president of the United States (1933-1945). Page 39.

principles: fundamental truths, laws or motivating forces, upon which others are based. Page 14.

privation: lack of the basic necessities or comforts of life. Also, the condition resulting from such lack. Page 68.

process: prepare raw materials for market, manufacture or other use by treating them in a series of operations that changes them. Page 54.

process: a systematic and technically exact series of steps, actions or changes to bring about a specific and definite result. In Scientology, a precise series of techniques or exercises applied by a practitioner to help a person find out more about himself and his life and to improve his condition. Page 97.

processed: received *processing,* an action composed of a precise series of techniques or exercises applied by a Scientology practitioner to help a person find out more about himself and his life and to improve his condition. Page 89.

propitiative: *propitiation* is a low emotion below anger and close to apathy. *Propitiative* means trying to please or satisfy someone in a way calculated to win their favor in order to defend or protect oneself against their disapproval, attack, etc. Page 88.

pummeling: pounding or beating, as with the fists. Used figuratively. Page 59.

punitive: inflicting, concerned with or directed toward punishment. Page 60.

purchase: an effective hold or position for applying power in moving or raising a heavy object or in preventing an object from slipping. Hence, a firm grip or grasp on something. Page 37.

purposes: intended or desired results; aims; goals. Page 26.

qualms: disturbing or uneasy feelings. Page 77.

rabble-rousers: people who stir up hatred, violence or other strong feelings in a group or a crowd through emotionalism, especially for political reasons. Page 20.

races (win at the): organized contests run over a regular course, such as horse racing or dog racing, where people bet money on a potential winner with the hope of attaining money. Page 21.

ramifications: results or consequences of something. Page 113.

random: proceeding, made or occurring without definite reason, method or pattern. Page 7.

rather: more accurately or correctly speaking; more truly. Page 5.

rats, study of: reference to the practice of psychologists and psychiatrists who study the behavior of rats in cages, hoping to apply their observations to humans. Page 14.

raw: brutal, harsh. Page 10.

raw materials: unprocessed natural products used in manufacture or production. Page 45.

reactive mind: the reactive mind is a stimulus-response mechanism. Ruggedly built and operable in trying circumstances, the reactive mind *never* stops operating. Pictures of a very low order are taken by this mind of the environment, even in some states of unconsciousness. The reactive mind acts *below* the level of consciousness. Page 74.

read into: find additional hidden or unintended meanings in something written or spoken. Page 70.

realm: an area or field of activity, thought, study or interest. Page 22.

rear: the part of a military force farthest from the fighting front. Page 106.

red revolution: a bloody, violent and radical revolution such as the 1917 Communist revolution that took place in Russia wherein the existing government was forcefully taken over and replaced with a Communist government led by Vladimir Lenin (1870-1924). The word *red* not only suggests violence but refers to a political radical or revolutionary, especially a Communist, since their regimes are usually accompanied with bloodshed. Page 10.

refrain: to hold back, keep oneself from doing something. Page 74.

regime: a form of government or rule; political system. Also, a system, especially one imposed by a government. Page 19.

rehabilitate: restore to a good condition or operation. Page 78.

remunerative: paying money; profitable. Page 36.

renders: causes to be or become; makes. Page 73.

resigns himself: submits quietly without complaint; accepts something as impossible to avoid or prevent. Page 73.

resorts: goes to or falls back on someone or something in time of need; turns to for aid or relief. Page 21.

restimulated: reactivated; stimulated again. *Re-* means again and *stimulate* means to bring into action or activity. Page 74.

rise: increase in fortune or rank, especially in one's job or position with an accompanying increase in salary; advance towards a flourishing or prosperous condition. Page 6.

riveted: fixed or held firmly. Page 110.

run out: to get rid of or exhaust the negative influence of something. Page 113.

ruts: patterns or ways of life that have become uninteresting and tiresome but are hard to change. Page 10.

sacked: dismissed or discharged from employment; fired. Page 12.

saddled: burdened or loaded with. Page 105.

sake: interest or benefit. Page 122.

save: with the exception of; except. Page 74.

scant: barely sufficient in amount; inadequate in amount. Page 6.

scheme of things: an overall organized system within which everything has a place. Page 39.

schemes: large-scale systematic plans or arrangements for attaining some particular object or putting a particular idea into effect. Page 56.

science: knowledge; comprehension or understanding of facts or principles, classified and made available in work, life or the search for truth. A science is a connected body of demonstrated truths or observed facts systematically organized and bound together under general laws. It includes trustworthy methods for the discovery of new truth within its domain and denotes the application of scientific methods in fields of study previously considered open only to theories based on subjective, historical or undemonstrable, abstract criteria. The word *science,* when applied to Scientology, is used in this sense—the most fundamental meaning and tradition of the word—and not in the sense of the *physical* or *material* sciences. Page 1.

scope: the range covered by a subject or topic. Page 62.

score: twenty people or things; set of twenty. Page 6.

scorned: rejected someone with extreme disfavor, sometimes with the idea of looking down upon them. Page 6.

set: to establish for others to follow; furnish as a pattern or model. Page 123.

shaken up: upset by or as if by a physical jolt or shock. Page 47.

sheerest: completely; without qualification. Page 123.

shocks: sudden and violent physical blows or impacts; collisions; any sudden disturbances or agitations of the mind or emotions, as through great loss or surprise. Page 106.

short of: without going to the point of or so far as. Page 107.

shortsighted: 1. unable to see beyond one's immediate surroundings, conditions, situations, etc. Page 70.
2. not able to see far. Page 110.

shying away: drawing back or avoiding. Page 109.

slander: a false and intentionally harmful statement that damages somebody's reputation. Page 8.

slashed: cut one's way using sweeping strokes with or as if with a sharp instrument. Used figuratively. Page 123.

sphere: a field of activity or operation. Page 60.

spikes, sitting on: a reference to the practice in some Eastern religious orders of sitting or lying on a board covered with spikes or nails in the belief that spiritual benefit is gained through suffering pain or discomfort. Page 14.

sport: fun or play. A *sport* is an activity involving physical skill that is governed by a set of rules or customs and often undertaken competitively and enjoyed by those participating. Page 73.

stable: firmly established; solid; fixed. *Stable* derives from Latin *stabilis* meaning firm, steadfast. Page 22.

stalked: walked angrily and stiffly. Page 27.

stamps: slang term for money (usually paper money). Page 7.

stand: to put up with patiently; endure or tolerate. Page 10.

stand up to: to meet or deal with; to confront or face up to. Page 22.

steadied: made firmer in position or place; made freer from change or variation. Page 24.

stem: arise or originate from, or be caused by something or someone. Page 92.

stenographer: one who is a specialist in the skill or work of writing down dictation in shorthand and later transcribing it, as on a typewriter. (*Shorthand* is a fast method of writing, using symbols to represent letters, words or groups of words.) Page 6.

stepped forward: presented oneself, as if by taking a single step, and entered into an activity or situation to set about doing something. Page 28.

still: (used to emphasize a comparison) in addition; even more; yet. Page 6.

storm: a disturbance in the air above the Earth, involving strong winds and usually rain (sometimes with lightning and thunder), snow, sleet or hail. Hence, any (violent) disturbance or upheaval in political, social or domestic affairs. Page 20.

studiously: with considerable attention; deliberately. Page 122.

stunted: stopped, slowed down or hindered (said of growth or development). Page 104.

subordinates: persons under the authority or control of another within an organization. Page 55.

sun, under the: in the world; on Earth. Page 14.

supper club: a restaurant serving fancy evening meals and sometimes featuring entertainment. Page 6.

sweat, in a: working very hard to achieve something; overworking. Page 6.

sweeping: wide in range or effect; general. Page 19.

swing through it: a reference to the motion of a boxer hitting or punching with a swinging motion of the arm(s). Hence, to battle one's way through something conceived of as threatening or attacking. Page 20.

switchboard: the central part of a telephone system used by a company where telephone calls are answered and connected (switched) to the appropriate person or department. Page 21.

symptoms: conditions that accompany something and indicate its existence; signs. Page 5.

teeth, gritting one's: summoning up one's strength to face unpleasantness or overcome a difficulty. *Grit* is used here in the sense of both clamping one's teeth together and grinding them with effort. Page 21.

terminal(s): anything that can receive, relay or send a communication. This term comes from the field of electronics where a terminal is one of two fixed points between which a flow of energy travels. An example of this is a car battery which has two connecting posts (terminals) where energy flows from one post to the other. In Scientology, two people communicating are called terminals because communication flows between them. Page 85.

thumbs, all: lacking physical coordination, skill or grace; clumsy or awkward, as if one's hands contained all thumbs and no fingers. Page 6.

timid: lacking in self-assurance; fearful and hesitant. Page 39.

tinsel path: *tinsel* is a thread, strip of paper, plastic or metal used to produce a sparkling or glittery effect. Used figuratively to mean something marked by a deceptively brilliant or valuable appearance. Hence a *tinsel path* would be an attractive course of action or conduct with little real worth or value. Page 20.

titanic: of enormous size, strength or power; gigantic. From the Greek myth of giant deities who sought to rule heaven and were overthrown. Page 67.

to hand: nearby or close; in plain sight or obvious. Page 72.

toil: hard and continuous work; exhausting labor or effort. Page 8.

tone: a particular mental state or disposition; spirit, character or mood. Page 68.

Tone Scale: a scale of emotional tones which shows the levels of human behavior. The Tone Scale is fully described in Chapter Six. Page 89.

tools of (one's) trade: those things needed to do one's job. Page 46.

torrent: uncontrolled outpouring, likened to a violent, swift-flowing stream. Page 7.

true-blue: unwaveringly loyal or faithful. Page 28.

tumbling: disordered, confused or disarranged, likened to something rolling or tossed about. Page 7.

turns loose: lets go, releases. Page 21.

tyranny: a government in which a single ruler has absolute power and uses it unjustly or cruelly. Page 10.

under someone's immediate nose: a variation of *under someone's nose,* plainly visible, in full view of, sometimes implying without the person himself perceiving it. The use of the word *immediate* intensifies the phrase and in this sense means near or close at hand. Page 72.

union(s): short for *labor union,* an organization of wage earners that is set up to serve and advance its members' interests in terms of wages, benefits, working hours and working conditions. Page 33.

Universal Military Training: a system under which all qualified citizens of a country are required to serve as military personnel in one of the armed forces for a specified length of time. *Universal* in this sense means affecting, concerning or involving all. Page 104.

unknownness: the state or condition of not knowing. Page 12.

unpositive: lacking certainty. Page 46.

unsettled: made uneasy or disturbed; made uncertain or unstable. Page 62.

untutored: having had no formal education or instruction. Page 6.

upscale: higher on the Tone Scale. Page 93.

Vedic Hymns: the earliest learned writings of which we have any record on Earth. They are the most ancient sacred literature of the Hindus comprising over a hundred books still in existence. They tell about evolution, about Man coming into this universe and the curve of life which is birth, growth, degeneration and decay. Page 48.

vengeance, with a: to an extreme degree; in an intense manner. Page 113.

verve: lively vigorous spirit, excitement or energy. Page 107.

vested interest: special interest in something for particular personal reasons. Page 114.

virtue of, by: by reason of; as a result of. Page 33.

"waiting for something to turn up": a reference to a philosophy of life displayed by the character Mr. Wilkins Micawber, from the well-known nineteenth-century novel *David Copperfield,* by English author Charles Dickens (1812–1870). Micawber, a friend of Copperfield's, comes up with many ideas to bring about wealth, and although his attempts fail, he never gives up and remains certain something will "turn up." Page 21.

wake, in (one's): *wake* is the visible trail (of agitated and disturbed water) left by something, such as a ship, moving through water. Hence, a condition left behind someone or something that has passed; following as a consequence. Page 26.

warped: turned from the true, natural or right course or direction. Page 105.

washed (one's) hands of: refused to have any further connection with; disclaimed any further responsibility for. Page 86.

watery: suggestive of water, as in being thin, pale or liquid. Page 94.

172

welfare state(s): a political system in which a government assumes the primary burden for its citizens such as by paying them directly when out of work or financially supporting their health needs. Page 33.

Western: of or pertaining to the countries and people of Europe and the Americas. Page 14.

wherein: in regard to which. Page 6.

wherewithal: the necessary means, especially financial ones, required for a purpose. Page 10.

wise: 1. knowledgeable and experienced persons. Page 6.
2. way or manner. Page 48.

with a large hand: from the phrase *helping hand* which means to give aid or assistance to someone. Hence, *with a large hand* is assistance of great quantity affecting many. Page 117.

with a vengeance: to an extreme degree; in an intense manner. Page 113.

withstanding: opposing, resisting or enduring, especially in a successful way. Page 57.

wits: intelligence, reasoning power. Page 7.

workaday: belonging to or characteristic of a workday or its occupations; characterized by a regular succession or round of tasks and jobs; of ordinary everyday life. Page 1.

work, close: carrying out a task, series of steps, etc., in a tight working relationship. Page 107.

worth: the value of one's material possessions; wealth. Page 12.

yesteryear: in the past, often a period with a set of values or a way of life that no longer exists. Page 123.

young 'un: young one. Page 6.

zest: great enthusiasm and energy. Page 34.

INDEX

extroversion, 107–117

> after handling people all
> day, 113
>
> cure for labor difficulties,
> 116
>
> definition, 107
>
> description, 109
>
> extroverted personality, 107
>
> importance of, 113
>
> principle of introversion–
> extroversion, 117
>
> through use of disrelated
> task, 116

extroverted personality

> definition, 107

F

"fall of physical energy," 112

family

> connection, jobs and, 5
>
> money and raising a, 104
>
> one-tenth of life, 11

fear

> chronically in, 92
>
> illustrated, 90
>
> tone improves to anger, 91

firm

> best interests of the, 96
>
> careless of the, 5
>
> solutions to save, 7
>
> taking out of the, 40

fixation

> of attention
>
>> cure for, 111
>>
>> on people, 114
>
> on one of the factors of
> control, 56
>
> tiredness and attention, 110

football

> game and control, 73

foreman, 70

> bad control by, 26
>
> bringing order, 24
>
> declining control of, 59
>
> doing everything, 55
>
> emergencies and confusion
> of, 22
>
> inventing personalities for
> workers, 70
>
> lacking understanding of
> situation, 59
>
> son becoming the, 5

franticness, 54

> inability to
> start-change-and-stop
> and, 61

freedom, 68

> game and, 73
>
> right to work versus
> pretended, 34

fun

> less than a spirit of, 74
>
> living and, 67

inability

    to pay attention to own job, 76

incompetence, 54

    bad control and, 50

    men and, 75

Industrial Age, 11

industry, 5

    laziness versus, 6

inefficiency

    bad control and, 50

    definition, 72

    inability to control and, 54

injury, 122

    environment coincident with accident or, 110

    exhaustion and, 105

    from a machine, consequence, 77

    identifying tools with, 77

    incapable of control and, 76

    lodges in reactive mind, 74

    restimulation of, 74, 106

    worker not paying attention to, 91

insanity

    conditions of work and, 11

    contagious, 61

    denial of work and, 34

    remedy for, 36

insecurity

    absence of knowledge and, 12

    chaos of data and, 11

    definition, 12

    spread around, 40

    unknownness and, 12

intelligence, 5, 7

    definition, 25

    holding a job and, 7

    raise, 123

    related to ability, 121

    Scientology can increase, 14

intention

    control and, 26

    failure of, 97

    of life toward objects, 50

interest

    below apathy and no, 91

    holding a job and, 5, 7

    in a job or in life, 63

    in our work condemned, 7

    total prediction and no real, 67

    unpredictability and, 72

introversion, 107–117

    definition, 107

    exhaustion and, 109

    introverted personality, 107, 109

    labor disputes and, 116

    principle of introversion-extroversion, 117

introversion-extroversion, 107–117

introverted personality, 109

definition, 107

J

job

ability to hold, 121

attempted control far beyond one's, 63

automation and providing many new jobs, 35

bad mental condition and no, 11

control and a good, 75

detesting a, 39

failed to control more than their own, 75

game and, illustration, 69

having no, 8

holding one depends on, 5–15

inventing new, 35

is a game, 68

loss of, 33

only way to hold, 40

promotion, 7

right versus no right to have, 36

secret of doing a good, 62

security of, 14

stable datum, 27–29

start-change-and-stop, 55

any part of, 62

example of, 59

under own determinism, 58

juvenile delinquency, 104

K

knowingness

good control and, 50

see also **knowledge**

knowledge

insecurity and absence of, 12

job security and, 14

stable datum and body of, 24

see also **knowingness**

L

labor, 115–117

child labor

abuse of, 104

laws, 34

management relations, 117

management versus, 70

perform honest, 122

reason for troubles, 115–116

laborers

environmental control, 45

importance of, 124

management and, 55

opponent

member of team and, 71

necessary to a game, 68

obsessive need of, 70

uncontrolled factor, 73

order

bringing, 24

organization

below apathy, liability to, 91

rational, 71

running in agreement with itself, 60

seeking to spread insecurity in, 40

"overloafed," 40

overstrained, 114–116

"overworked," 40

P

past

failure now due to failure in, 76

paycheck

go through motions and draw, 39

more to work than, 36

struggle for, 11

work for its own sake versus, 122

pension, 19

people

ability to control, 121

remedy after handling people all day, 113

simply look at, 114

personal ability, 5

personal charm

holding a job and, 5, 6

play

definition, 35

endless, 36

game, and return ability to, 123

work versus, 35

pleasure, 68

politics

one-tenth of life, 11

prediction, 67

of what a person will do, 89

present time

working in, 78

problems

confusion and, 20, 29

game and necessity of, 68

lacking and inventing, 70

national insanity, 11

of control, 45

person lacking, 70

process

Look Them Over, 113

S

salesman, 114

sanity

  person versus environment, 60

  positive control and, 52

  right to work and, 34

science

  of life, 1, 14

Science of Survival, 95

Scientology, 15, 68, 98

  handling of exhaustion, 106

  increase ability and, 123

  many applications of, 1

  organization in agreement with itself, 60

  practitioner, 75

  science of life, 1, 14

  subjects of introversion and extroversion, and, 107

  Tone Scale of, 89

second wind

  definition, 113

secret of efficiency, 45–63

security

  definition, 25

  goal of working man, 8

  job and, 14

  part of life, 11

  quest for, 10

  undermine one's, 20

  understanding and, 12

self-confidence, 75

serenity, 91

  illustrated, 90

  value of, 92

shortsighted, 110

sleep, really relaxing, 113

society, 58

  being part of, 105

  denial of work and revenge on, 35

  neurosis in, 33

  nonproductive, criminal, 117

  people that stop and, 57

  work is stable datum of, 122

solidity

  reality and, 93

    solids, 109

space

  affinity and, 94

stable datum, 27

  adopted, not necessarily true, 28

  being a, 61

  confusion and shaking, 27, 28

  doctrine of, 22, 27

  holding a job and, 27, 29

  invalidated, 29, 40

  opposite side of doctrine of, 27

  start-change-and-stop and, 53

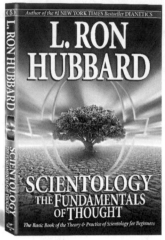